BULLETIN OF THE JOHN RYLANDS LIBRARY

The Artist of the Future Age: William Blake, Neo-Romanticism, Counterculture and Now

Guest Editors: Douglas Field and Luke Walker

VOLUME 98 NUMBER 1, SPRING 2022

BULLETIN OF THE JOHN RYLANDS LIBRARY

ISSN 2054-9318 (Print)
ISSN 2054-9326 (Online)

Established in 1903

Subscriptions

To subscribe please contact: Manchester University Press Journals Subscriptions,
176 Waterloo Place, University of Manchester, Oxford Road,
Manchester, M13 9GP, UK
Tel: +44 (0)161 275 2310
manchesterhive@manchester.ac.uk
https://www.manchesterhive.com/view/journals/bjrl/bjrl-overview.xml

The *Bulletin* is published twice a year. The subscription prices for 2022 are:
Institutions (print and online) £215/$325/€255
Institutions (online only) £179/$265/€205
Individual (print only) £73/$110/€83

The complete archive of the *Bulletin of the John Rylands Library*, from its first issue in 1903 to Volume 80 (1998) is now available to purchase from Manchester University Press. The archive complements the current subscription product (1999 to date), and can be purchased on a one-time basis or as an annual subscription. To obtain pricing information, please contact Shelly Turner at shelly.turner@manchester.ac.uk.

BULLETIN OF THE JOHN RYLANDS LIBRARY

VOLUME 98 NUMBER 1, SPRING 2022

The Artist of the Future Age: William Blake, Neo-Romanticism, Counterculture and Now

CONTENTS

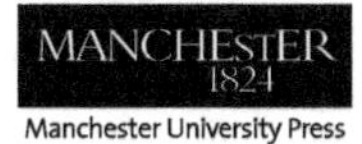

Introduction

DOUGLAS FIELD, UNIVERSITY OF MANCHESTER
LUKE WALKER, UNIVERSITY OF ROEHAMPTON

As we were drafting this introduction, we heard the sad news of the death of one of our contributors, the poet Michael Horovitz (1935–2021). His lifelong commitment to William Blake is reflected in his written and artistic contributions to this collection, including what turned out to be his final piece of writing, which is published in this special issue. As a mainstay of British counterculture, Horovitz's work is also discussed in several of the articles by other contributors. We would therefore like to dedicate this issue to his memory.

In memoriam Michael Horovitz (4 April 1935–7 July 2021)

This special issue, 'The Artist of the Future Age: William Blake, Neo-Romanticism, Counterculture and Now', has its origins in the conference of the same name which took place in the John Rylands Library in October 2019, featuring many of the present contributors. The illumination cast by the stained glass windows in the neo-Gothic space of the Historic Reading Room created a fitting atmosphere for talks (and in the case of Horovitz, also songs) on the visionary Blake and his legacy, but the more immediate inspiration for the symposium came from the serendipitous combination of texts to be found in this research library. The John Rylands Library holds a number of original engraved works by Blake, including a very rare hand-coloured copy of his illustrations to Edward Young's *Night Thoughts* (1797), as well as a copy of Blake's final completed publication, the *Illustrations of the Book of Job* (1826). While Blake's genius was little appreciated in his own time, it seems appropriate that alongside these works, the library also holds important collections associated with the later movement for which Blake became a presiding spirit, namely the British counterculture of the 1960s and 1970s.

Among these countercultural holdings at the John Rylands Library are the archives of Dave Cunliffe (1941–2021) and of Jeff Nuttall (1933–2004), whose 1968 book *Bomb Culture* – an insider's account of the origins and key events of the British counterculture – is peppered with references to Blake. Nuttall drew attention to Blake's revolutionary figure of Orc as an animating spirit of the 1960s, and memorably described the Blakean energy catalysed by the International Poetry Incarnation of 1965: 'London is in flames', he wrote immediately after the momentous Albert Hall poetry event, 'the Spirit of William Blake walks on the water of Thames'.[1]

Bulletin of the John Rylands Library, Volume 98, No. 1 (Spring 2022), pp. 1–5, published by Manchester University Press.
http://dx.doi.org/10.7227/BJRL.98.1.1

It has often been noted that there was a certain amount of tension between the British and American poets at the Albert Hall, and it is even possible to link some of this to the disputed 'ownership' of Blake.[2] This dynamic is complicated further if we consider that much of Blake's own work – and his Albion myth in particular – also embodies a tension between the contraries of nationalism and internationalism.[3] However, there can be little doubt that the shared interest in Blake was also an important bridge between the countercultures on either side of the Atlantic. It is equally clear that Blake provided a point of connection or continuity between the 1960s, within which the term 'counterculture' was coined, and earlier movements which might equally be described as countercultural. These range from Romanticism itself to other avant-gardes of the nineteenth and twentieth centuries, some of which are discussed in this issue. Neither can we ignore the ongoing (counter)cultural influence of Blake, as discussed in the concluding article, which explores the ways in which his spirit infuses a contemporary Belgian experimental arts collective. Other signs of the ever-expanding cultural impact of Blake include the huge publicity generated by the 2019 Blake exhibition at Tate Britain, and more recently by John Higgs's book, *William Blake vs the World* (2021), an unashamedly proselytising introduction to Blake's ideas, aimed at a popular audience.

Just as popular interest in Blake is blossoming, so is the scholarly sub-genre of Blakean reception studies. The origins of this field date back to Deborah Dorfman's *Blake in the Nineteenth Century: His Reputation as a Poet from Gilchrist to Yeats* (1969), eventually followed by Robert J. Bertholf and Annette S. Levitt's collection *William Blake and the Moderns* (1982). Now, in the twenty-first century, this field has finally burst into flower, with monographs including Edward Larrissy's *Blake and Modern Literature* (2006) and Colin Trodd's *Visions of Blake: William Blake in the Art World 1830–1930* (2012), and edited collections such as *Blake 2.0: William Blake in Twentieth-Century Art, Music and Culture* (eds Steve Clark, Tristanne Connolly and Jason Whittaker, 2012), *Blake, Modernity and Popular Culture* (eds Steve Clark and Jason Whittaker, 2007), *The Reception of Blake in the Orient* (eds Steve Clark and Masashi Suzuki, 2006), and *The Reception of William Blake in Europe* (eds Sibylle Erle and Morton D. Paley, 2019). Several other recent or forthcoming books focus specifically on Blake's American reception, with a notable emphasis on counterculture: these include *William Blake and the Age of Aquarius* (an illustrated catalogue of essays accompanying the 2017 exhibition at Northwestern University's Block Museum, edited by Stephen F. Eisenman), Linda Freedman's *William Blake and the Myth of America: From the Abolitionists to the Counterculture* (2018), and Luke Walker's forthcoming *William Blake and Allen Ginsberg: Romanticism, Counterculture and Radical Reception*.

In gathering the collection of articles in this special issue, our intention has therefore been to further expand this blossoming field of Blake reception studies, in this case with a specific focus on Blake's British and European reception from the late nineteenth century to the present day, and an understanding that Blake's countercultural aspect lies at the centre of that reception history, radiating in all directions. While there is much to commend about the volume *William Blake and the Age of*

Aquarius – in which Blake's influence on American artists, among them Jay DeFeo, Jim Morrison and Bob Dylan, is discussed – the contributors do not consider the ways that British artists such as Michael Horovitz, Iain Sinclair and Jeff Nuttall were also animated by the nineteenth-century poet. This special issue seeks to remind readers that Blake's prophetic vision and antinomian spirit was also central to many British and Irish writers from the early to mid-twentieth century.

With this in mind, we begin by reprinting the essay Michael Horovitz wrote to commemorate Blake's 1957 bicentenary, first published in *Oxford Opinion* the following year. Entitled 'The Blake Renaissance', Horovitz's article observes that Blake has been claimed or dismissed by successive generations since his death in 1827. For the Romantics, he was a 'weird crank', while the Victorians enveloped the poet-painter in 'their own damp sentimentalism'. As Horovitz explains, Blake 'evades appraisal because he was always working for a synthesis of creation far beyond outward forms and *genres*', which meant that 'he had to invent his own methods to express himself adequately'. Horovitz notes that the recent bicentenary was marked by 'floods of exhibitions, magazine supplements, radio features, new books from all sides devoted to him'. This clearly anticipates the Blakean explosion of the 1960s, in which Horovitz himself would play a major role. Written shortly before he abandoned his postgraduate studies at Oxford (on Blake) to found the magazine *New Departures* and hit the road as a Beat poet, Horovitz's essay can therefore be seen as marking the beginning of Sixties Blake in Britain.

In the conclusion of 'The Blake Renaissance', Horovitz noted how 'everything Blake did has its significance for us today', adding that 'some of his most pertinent prophecies are insufficiently understood in our time'. Horovitz's newly written (and final) essay, 'William Blake & (a few of) his Friends in Our Time', charts the continuation of his fascination with the figure he would call 'Great Grandfather William', from the 1960s – when his friend Jeff Nuttall described Blake's spirit walking on the waters of the Thames – to the final months of his life.

For the writer W. B. Yeats, the spirit of Blake also walked on the waters of Innisfree during the 1890s. As Jodie Marley explores in '"Invisible Gates Would Open": W. B. Yeats and William Blake in the 1890s', the Irish writer co-authored the three volumes of *The Works of William Blake: Poetic, Symbolic, and Critical* (1893) with Edwin Ellis. Yeats paved the way for later scholars and artists who, like him, were drawn to the esoteric and spiritual dimensions of Blake's life and work. By insisting that Blake must be read alongside certain writers, among them the Swedish theologian Emanuel Swedenborg, Marley shows the way that Yeats helped to shape Blake's critical legacy.

In 'William Blake and the Spiritual Forms of Citizenship and Hospitality', Colin Trodd focuses on the reception of the poet-painter between 1910 and 1930. Drawing on unstudied material, Trodd charts the ways that Blake's legacy during this period became an ideological battleground where commentators jostled for their version of Blake. Whereas Yeats foregrounded the prophetic nature of the Romantic artist, Blake later became embroiled in debates about citizenship, raising key questions about the political and ontological value of his work. 'Was it possible', Trodd

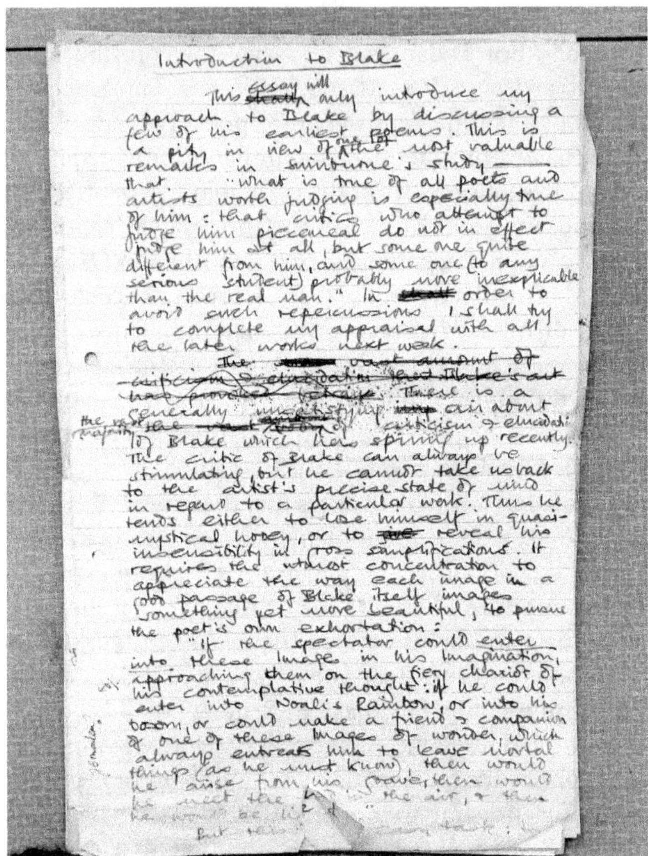

Introduction to Blake

This essay will only introduce my approach to Blake by discussing a few of his earliest poems. This is a pity in view of one of the most valuable remarks in Swinburne's study — that "what is true of all poets and artists worth judging is especially true of him: that critics who attempt to judge him piecemeal do not in effect judge him at all, but some one quite different from him, and some one (to any serious student) probably more inexplicable than the real man." In order to avoid such repercussions I shall try to complete my appraisal with all the later works next week.

There is a generally mystifying air about the vast majority of criticism & elucidation of Blake which has sprung up recently. The critic of Blake can always be stimulating, but he cannot take us back to the artist's precise state of mind in regard to a particular work. Thus he tends either to lose himself in quasi-mystical hokey, or to reveal his insensibility in gross simplifications. It requires the utmost concentration to appreciate the way each image in a good passage of Blake itself images something yet more beautiful, to pursue the poet's own exhortation:

"If the spectator could enter into these images in his imagination, approaching them on the fiery chariot of his contemplative thought: if he could enter into Noah's Rainbow, or into his bosom, or could make a friend & companion of one of these images of wonder, which always entreats him to leave mortal things (as he must know), then would he arise from his grave, then would he meet the [illegible] the air, & then he would be [illegible]

Figure 1 First page of the manuscript of Michael Horovitz's article 'The Blake Renaissance', recently discovered among the author's papers. Photo: Vanessa Vie.

asks in relation to these debates, 'for the modern artist to create individual critical works which combined cognitive mastery of aesthetic form with moral integrity of aesthetic experience?'

In 'Avant-Garde Blake: From Francis Bacon to *Oz* Magazine', David Hopkins explores Blake's avant-garde reception. Beginning with a discussion of Peter Bürger's influential theorisation of the avant-garde, Hopkins analyses Francis Bacon's series of portraits that were made from Blake's life mask. The essay then explores the ways that Blake was utilised in a number of left-wing little magazines to comment on political issues that were central to the 1960s counterculture. Blake, as Hopkins points out, became a central figure around which debates about the counterculture and the avant-garde turned.

Blake's importance to the British counterculture is explored further by James Riley in 'Iain Sinclair, William Blake and the Visionary Poetry of the 1960s'. While a number of writers associated with the underground scene of the 1960s drew on Blake as a visionary, Riley explores Iain Sinclair's 'topographic take' on the

Romantic poet. As Riley shows, Blake has been a central figure in the development of Sinclair's metropolitan psychogeography. By analysing the work of Michael Horovitz and the poet Harry Fainlight, both of whom channelled Blake in different ways, Riley shows how the writers he discusses 'point to the plurality of Blake as a figure of influence and the variation underpinning his literary utility in post-1960s poetry'.

In '"The Place Where Contrarieties are Equally True": Blake and the Science-Fiction Counterculture', Jason Whittaker explores the ways that 'a more detached and ironic' view of Blake emerged in the 1970s. Focusing on three science-fiction novels – Ray Nelson's *Blake's Progress* (1977), Angela Carter's *The Passion of New Eve* (1977), and J. G. Ballard's *The Unlimited Dream Company* (1979) – Whittaker explores the ways in which all three works share reservations about the counterculture of the previous decade. In contrast to the counterculture of the 1960s, during which time Blake was an unambiguously positive figure, he later emerges in an ambivalent light.

The special issue concludes with 'A Cosmopolitan Case Study: Countercultural Blake in the Therapoetic Practice of maelstrÖm reEvolution', in which Franca Bellarsi tracks the reception of Blake's countercultural legacy through maelstrÖm reEvolution, the Brussels-based experimental performance and arts collective. Drawing on interviews and new material, Bellarsi reads Blake as 'the archetypal embodiment of the shamanic poet' through maelstrÖm's 'therapoetic' experimentalism which underscores the ways that Blake's work continues to reinvigorate and challenge contemporary transnational art and poetics.

As editors, we would like to thank all our contributors, who worked on these articles during the challenging circumstances of the pandemic. Special thanks are owed to Colin Trodd, who in addition to contributing an article was the primary organiser of the original symposium; also to our anonymous peer reviewer, whose enthusiasm for the project, careful reading and thoughtful suggestions were invaluable.

Notes

1 Jeff Nuttall, *Bomb Culture*, eds Douglas Field and Jay Jeff Jones (London: Strange Attractor, 2018), p. 195.

2 See Luke Walker, 'Beat Britain: Poetic Vision and Division in Albion's "Underground"', in *The Routledge Handbook of International Beat Literature*, ed. A. Robert Lee (New York: Routledge, 2018), pp. 45–57.

3 See Luke Walker, 'Allen Ginsberg's Blakean Albion', *Comparative American Studies*, 11 (2013), 227–42.

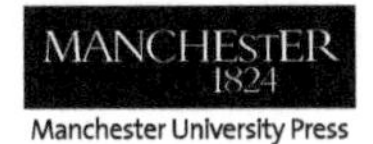

The Blake Renaissance

MICHAEL HOROVITZ

(Originally published in *Oxford Opinion*, 'Special Art Issue', Hilary Term 1958)

Abstract

This article, originally published in 1958, was written to commemorate William Blake's bicentenary. In it, the author observes that Blake has been claimed or dismissed by successive generations since his death in 1827: for the Romantics, he was a 'weird crank', while the Victorians enveloped him in 'their own damp sentimentalism'. The author argues that Blake 'evades appraisal because he was always working for a synthesis of creation far beyond outward forms and *genres*', which meant 'he had to invent his own methods to express himself adequately'. He notes that the recent bicentenary was marked by 'floods of exhibitions, magazine supplements, radio features, new books from all sides devoted to him'. This clearly anticipates the Blakean explosion of the 1960s, in which the author himself would play a major role. This article can therefore be seen as marking the beginning of Sixties Blake in Britain.

Keywords: William Blake; Blake bicentenary; W. H. Auden; *The Marriage of Heaven and Hell*; Max Plowman; Kathleen Raine

Last year saw the bicentenary of William Blake ostentatiously celebrated as something more and less than a revival. Floods of exhibitions, magazine supplements, radio features, new books from all sides devoted to him, not least the Epstein bust ironically marked his first real *arrival.* Such loud bangs for Blake's birthday were welcome after the accumulated whimpers of previous generations. He has been fashionable in this century as an ephemeral cult, an *enfant terrible* in circles eclectic and exegetic; his 'character' among English artists is habitually abused as a dead cert to relieve the tedium of artcrit, and to colour lesser *Angst* and 'The Horse's Mouth'. Most of the Victorians who noticed his work engulfed it in their own damp sentimentalism. The Romantics regarded him as a weird crank: Wordsworth called the *Songs of Innocence and Experience* 'work of insane genius', but he was careful to put Blake on a special shelf: 'There is something in the madness of this man which interests me more than the sanity of Lord Byron and Walter Scott.' Blake displays a totally different kind of understanding in saying of Wordsworth, 'I cannot think that real poets have any competition. None are greatest in the Kingdom of God. It is so in poetry.' Blake cannot be assessed for our approved categories because he subjects himself to the universe of *spiritual* legislation only. The comparative standards give way before one who does not compete.

Although his great myths still lie relatively unexplored the legends of insanity still persist; the friendly guise of such as Professor Auden – who prefers the word 'dotty' because of its 'affectionate overtones' – serves to cover the superficial approach. This began in Blake's own time through his isolation from his contemporaries, his disgust for the mental urbanity in which Reynolds and Dr Johnson fettered themselves:

> Great things are done when men and mountains meet;
> This is not done by jostling in the street.

Pater deduces 'an instance of preponderating soul, embarrassed, at a loss in an era of preponderating mind'. This emphasis could mislead the modern reader of Blake. His *attitude* to the climate was radically different from that of the disciples of winking, blinking Sam (compare the two poems called 'London'), but he was far from being out of touch with it. He simply resorted to a visionary plane of being which enabled him to discard external nature as anything more than a medium towards the realm of imagination. The dramatisation of visions puzzles the unimaginative, and Blake was treated with the same brand of suspicion awarded to St Joan, the Lawrences, etc. His untrammelled imagination operated freely to the extinction of pressures on behalf of 'the Vegetable universe'. As he had luckily escaped any form of formal education his child's perception grew unclouded by alien indoctrination or organisation of ideas, and he remained all his life the sole director of his thought. So Blake uniquely trained his imagination to project the vision of his inner eye into the crater of phenomena. For him 'The Imagination is not a state: it is the Human Existence itself' – and for him there is no distinction between the Human and the Divine. How far Blake's immediate surroundings were cut off from this Existence is seen in his social squib *An Island in the Moon*: at the age of 30 he still felt the need to work off the inanities of blue-stocking salons, fashion whimsies, antiquarian quacks, eccentric philosophers and amateur philologists. He never returned to this side of London.

The renewed interest has aroused some purist carping, that Blake was not a 'good' painter or poet at all. He evades appraisal because he was always working for a synthesis of creation far beyond outward forms and *genres*. He knew 'I must create a System or be enslaved by another Man's':

> Thank God, I never was sent to school
> To be flogd into following the Style of a Fool.

So he had to invent his own methods to express himself adequately. He improvised various devices, notably the print-etched plate for printing in relief through which he disseminated the magnificent *Jerusalem* designs. Images and text were harmonised by drawing on metal with varnish and etching away the surface, in anticipation of modern techniques of photographic reproduction. It may be freely admitted that Blake's poetry and painting are rarely satisfactory as *such* – as his verse is often ungrammatical and badly measured, so his figures hardly fulfil the requirements of anatomy or rules of perspective. Blake is the type of inspiration, ever opposed to the clever effects of more consciously formulating minds. He is possessed by his intuitions, positive about every detail he records, a compulsive artist for whom the birth of an idea is its immediate execution. Certain of his personal vision, he couldn't bother with polishing his meter like Pope or slowly 'digesting, methodising' with Reynolds – 'He who does not know Truth at sight is unworthy of her notice.'

Blake served his apprenticeship as an engraver with seven years of copying which made him a fine craftsman. He admired Raphael, Michelangelo and the Gothic tombs in Westminster Abbey, and despised Dutch and Flemish naturalism from the first. His intentions in painting were in line with his transcendental intimations:

> Shall painting be confined to the sordid drudgery of fac-simile [facsimile] representations of merely mortal and perishing substances and not be, as poetry and music are, elevated to its own sphere of invention and visionary conception? No, it shall not be so! Painting, as well as poetry and music, exists and exults in immortal thoughts.

Blake's whole life was given to the creation of songs, poems and pictures to crystallise his awareness of the infinite and the eternal. In common with the mediaeval Christian Scholastic view, the Far Eastern and that of Meister Eckhart, Blake finds poetry and all art to be religion, and religion art, not related but the same: 'Jesus and his (Apostles and) Disciples were all Artists' …

> A Poet, a Painter, a Musician, an Architect: the Man or Woman
>   who is not one of these is not a Christian.
> You must leave Fathers and Mothers and Houses and Lands if they
>   stand in the way of Art.
> Prayer is the study of Art.
> Praise is the Practice of Art.
> Fasting, etc., all relate to Art.
> The outward Ceremony is Antichrist.
> The Eternal Body of Man is The Imagination, that is, God himself,
>   The Divine Body, Jesus: we are his members.
> It manifests itself in his Works of Art (in Eternity All is Vision).

One of the few abstract definitions to fit Blake is Shelley's of poets as 'the unacknowledged legislators of the world'. He never supposed that the revelations of his imagination couldn't be shared by others, and saw his task as an artist to be the giving of form to his apprehensions of universal reality. In the light of this it is quite absurd to sneer at his painting as 'too literary', his poetry as 'extravagant' or 'didactic'. Yeats came to appreciate that 'the literary element in painting, the moral element in poetry, are the means whereby the two arts are accepted into the social order and become a part of life, and not things of the study and the exhibition'. There is always this awareness in Blake of his essential communion with the largest possible audience, and there is always communicated a real scale and sense of values. We speak of this last, as a label today – generally to convey abstract moral laws of Deism or Behaviourism of the kind Blake abhorred. His own mission, to see the eternal spiritual values, to build Jerusalem in England's pastures green, is implicit in his work as the constant motive force.

A man totally adequate to his humanity is a symbol in himself. Blake's *Song of Liberty* is that of Gandhi and Schweitzer: 'Everything that lives is holy.' It is a religious song, and a communal one, in the recognition that all life is interdependent:

> Everything that lives
> Lives not for itself alone.

Only *America* and *Europe* are headed 'A Prophecy' – in the sense of an exposition of fundamental historical principles, not of prediction. The revolutionary spirit kindled Blake, but he was not content to urge reform through the extant channels of Church and State, institutions and politics. Revolution meant saving for the earth a portion of the infinite, in the manner of a prophet scrutinising minute particulars until their significance emerged. The point of a prophet is that he sees better and farther than most people, his sight is foresight. Isaiah is a great imaginative poet, and so is Blake. Imagination is the eye of the soul. The greatest poetry is the ultimate truth perceived by the human soul. Blake discovered, 'I question not my corporeal or vegetative eye any more than I would question a window concerning a sight. I look through it and not with it'. The eyes are traditionally the windows of the soul, and this idea has a practical application to a seer such as Blake. A proper recognition of his unblinkered vision reveals his soul with the utmost clarity, casting light inside and out. But the eye cannot illuminate the imagination as long as it is fixed only on the material world; it has to see through this to the infinite life of which it is only a symbol. By marking the 'Influence of Natural Objects in calling forth and strengthening the Imagination in Boyhood and Early Youth', Wordsworth was doddering on the circumference of the universe to the heart of which Blake had penetrated: 'Natural objects always did and now do weaken, deaden or obliterate imagination in me.'

> I assert for myself that I do not behold the outward Creation and that to me it is hindrance and not Action; it is as the dirt upon my feet, No part of Me. 'What', it will be Question'd, 'When the Sun rises, do you not see a round disk of fire somewhat like a Guinea?' O no, no, I see an Innumerable company of the Heavenly host crying, 'Holy, Holy, Holy, is the Lord God Almighty.'

Blake sometimes appears inconsistent on this subject because he adjusts his emphasis from the tentative to the perversely aggressive according to the context; but in the ideal synthesis spiritual and material are fused. Heaven and Hell walk hand in hand.

For practical purposes Blake evolved four degrees of perception, each a rarefaction of the preceding one. Single vision is pure sensation, the sight of objects to which reason was added to produce twofold vision, intellectual comprehension or 'pure scientific thought'. Threefold vision resulted with the superaddition of sentience; hence the poetry of intellectual coordination of sense impressions (as in Marvell and Burns) without the power to perceive images of truth that are essentially independent of the senses. Blake's final order of illumination was pure consciousness, the faculty of fourfold vision at one with spiritual reality. And this is the great setback to a complete appreciation. As Max Plowman said:

> While everybody understands *some* part, nobody understands the whole of his work ... Blake strove to portray the whole of man. In so doing, of course, he portrayed his own soul. But the soul has depths and heights which are beyond the range of purely intellectual concepts. The body can be seen, measured, anatomized, analysed; but, despite the painful efforts of psychoanalysis, the soul is beyond such survey: it must be spiritually sensed and he who intends faithfully to portray that which has only infinite bounds, must be prepared to see his lines extending beyond the range of human knowledge into those realms where apprehension supplants intelligence. It is not to be thought that the limited understanding which suffices for things material is going to make a total comprehension of that which is confessedly beyond the range of matter.

The despised 'single vision and Newton's Sleep' is the sleep of reason. Newton is closely connected with the 'Ancient of Days', the anxious God of rational knowledge armed with heavy brass-bound books and iron pen, who represents Blake's view of the creation as the imposition of the materialism of Urizen. Single vision interprets, or rather explains 'Urizen' as a petulant 'Your reason': but Blake's figures work on many levels, and this one is certainly derived also from the Greek 'limiting power', to suggest further images of narrow-mindedness. Newton is depicted measuring, like the ancient, with the golden compasses from *Paradise Lost* in his left hand. Sense perception of the physical world can be weighed in the balance of reason and restraint, but only the Poetic or Prophetic Genius can convey eternal Beauty and Truth. Compasses smell of Mortality: 'He who sees the infinite in all things sees God. He who sees the ratio only sees himself only.' Newton is a guardian of the 'Philosophy of the Five Senses', the arch-materialist of mechanical laws, valuable only in giving visible form to error in the face of the divine imagination – like Voltaire, Rousseau, Locke, linguistic analysts and all clockwork systematisers

> - You throw the sand against the wind
> And the wind blows it back again.
> - And every sand becomes a gem
> Reflected in the beams divine;
> Blown back they blind the mocking eye,
> But still in Israel's path they shine.
> - The atoms of Democritus
> And Newton's Particles of Light
> Are sands upon the Red Sea shore,
> Where Israel's tents do shine so bright.

The popular faiths of our time, from that of the committed to the New Scientist's, are still comforting codes and disguises which are stepped into, and which likewise stand reproved by the individual conscience – 'Men forget that all Deities reside in the Human Breast.' And when Reason has lost his reason he is left with nothing, viz. the gloomy degradation of Blake's *Nebuchadnezzar*, utterly submerged by the material world. Only the continuous tradition of Israel's tents, of poetry and art, can save mankind from this oppression. The escape from rationalism is displayed by *Elijah*, the prophet handing his cloak of inspiration to Elisha, symbolising the poet who grasps eternal truth by means of his genius, reveals it and hands it on.

Blake is often still patronised by critics as a 'splendid maniac', an exception to prove the rules; he is too rarely extolled as an illustrator incarnate. He illustrated himself supremely, sacrificing nothing to conventional 'form' or 'life'. One of the rewards of reading Blake in the facsimile manuscripts is to observe the childlike way his pictures are fitted in with the line-lengths. The joys of Blake may strike an idiot negativism as obscure, yet they remain plain and right to uncorrupted responses:

> I am happy to find a Great Majority of Fellow Mortals who can Elucidate My Visions, and Particularly they have been Elucidated by Children, who have taken a greater delight in contemplating my pictures than I even hoped. Neither Youth nor Childhood is Folly or Incapacity. Some Children are Fools and so are some Old Men. But there is a vast Majority on the side of Imagination and Spiritual Sensation.

Blake was thoroughly self-educated: this made him coin new techniques for new subjects from the reservoir of a well-stocked mind; so far from Eliot's wild amateur of home-made materials, he was profoundly a craftsman, his mind's eye communicated through the work of his hands: 'My fingers emit sparks of fire with Expectation of my future labours.'

His stress on outline at the expense of shading is akin to the 'Primitives'; the 'Gothic' strain is uppermost in the frontispiece to 'Ahania', and another side of it in 'Hecate'. This print is the child's fantasy world retained, in the spirit of medieval symbols and the similar ones of Henri Rousseau and Chagall. The charm, humour and pathos of Blake's pictures amid their aesthetic limitations is often overlooked in our passionate canonisation – we tend in the same way to miss much of Donne and Skelton – though of course the condescension to 'naïve', 'grotesque', etc., can be overplayed too (as it sometimes is with Chaucer, Rousseau and Chagall).

The *Job* sketch was done twenty-five years before Blake's illustrations to the 'Book' (*c.*1819): it exemplifies what a few of his rapid, clean, confident strokes can do, what life and character and personal stamp they endow. The cowed comforters, distraught wife and perplexed Job look forward to Blake's adaptation; its crux – that 'The letter killeth/The Spirit giveth life' is stated here, as in all Blake's work.

The Punishment of the Thieves is a generalised treatment of Dante's pit. Blake reacted against the *Commedia*'s doctrine of retribution, but his own serpents of materialism are destroying Woman after having helped her to dominate man. The female represented moral law, a lower level than the free, creative spirit of the male for Blake. Hence this allegory of Woman after the Fall. Blake has drawn the figure of the standing woman in the centre from an engraving after Michelangelo's *Last Judgement* – a typically incongruous flourish. In his zest Blake enlisted many of the master's devices and dressed them with his own idiosyncrasies, giving his figures a strange power that is quite unlike anything on earth. And this is also the point about Blake's illustrations of Dante and the *Job* – that he always coloured any text he was dealing with by the strongest lineaments of his own interpretation; so his designs are a commentary in their own right.

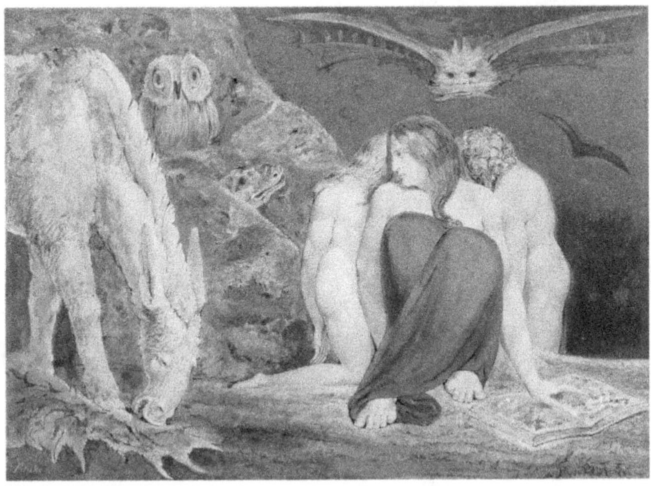

Figure 1 William Blake, *The Night of Enitharmon's Joy* (formerly called 'Hecate'), *c.*1795. Photo © Tate.

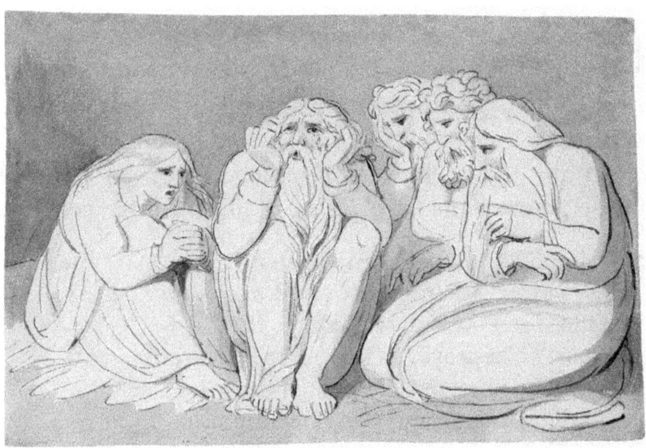

Figure 2 William Blake, *Job, his Wife and his Friends: The Complaint of Job*, *c.*1785. Photo: © Tate.

The theme of free will and destiny presented itself to Blake in the images of Heaven and Hell. First (*c.*1783) came his near-perfect image of free will – the *Songs of Innocence*, which was followed a little later by his equally vivid image of man under the shadow of destiny in the companion book of child-like drawings, the *Songs of Experience*. About ten years after this he propounded his synthesis of the contrary principles.[1] The *Songs* had expressed his ideas of good and evil as contrary states of the soul – many of the *Songs of Experience*, and especially the rejected ones in the Rossetti MS betray the resentment of the initial discovery of evil and its workings. In *The Marriage of Heaven and Hell* bitterness has been transmuted by

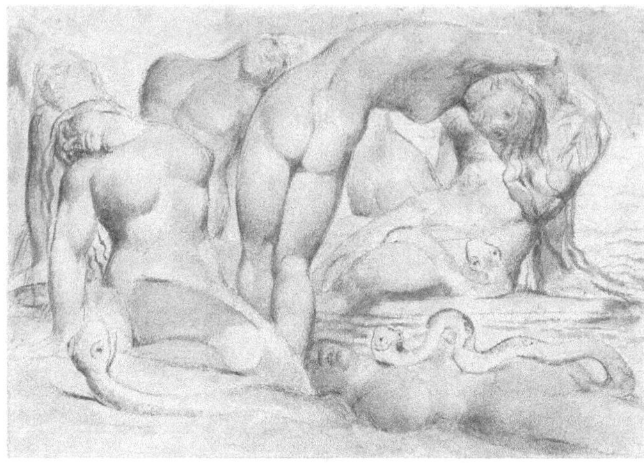

Figure 3 William Blake, *The Punishment of the Thieves*, illustration to Dante's *Divine Comedy*, 1824–27. Photo © Tate.

understanding. Evil is recognised as a state of experience through which the soul of man passed so that he could achieve a nobler state beyond the mere *Weltschmerz* of good and evil. Blake has triumphantly accepted his destiny by *The Marriage* – his joy is henceforth in the conflict for liberty and imagination, not in the shadow of Fate but revelling in the 'mental fight' which labours to 'build Jerusalem'. The purpose of pain discovered, the first victory of life is won in self-knowledge:

All that can be annihilated must be annihilated
That the Children of Jerusalem may be saved from slavery,
There is a Negation, and there is a Contrary:
The Negation must be destroyed to redeem the Contraries.
The Negation is the Spectre, the Reasoning power in man:
This is a false body, an Incrustation over my Immortal
Spirit, a Selfhood which must be put off and annihilated alway.
To cleanse the face of My Spirit by Self-examination,
To bathe in the Waters of Life, to wash off the Not Human,
I come in Self-annihilation and the grandeur of Inspiration.

This declaration put by Blake in the mouth of Milton is the next step – to wash off all the tyranny of reason, the presumption of selfhood, to become a conduit for the pure Imagination. It is a pity that there is still such widespread trepidation about reading Blake's longer poems – Auden finds them 'unreadable', and this is the word used by everyone about everything they have not made the effort to read. – Or intellectual self-respect is reinstated by 'fantastical' or 'mystic'. Kathleen Raine's comment is cogent:

> Let any poet invoke the names of Cupid or Phoebus and no one will question his claim to be speaking of these gods. But let a great poet recreate these figures

> and myths of Cupid and Phoebus, changing only the names, and few will recognise them. This is precisely what Blake has done. What he has attempted, in his prophetic writings, is to give a new expression, appropriate to eighteenth century industrial England, to the ageless figures of the gods.

The poems from *The Marriage* onward take the form of visionary treatises on contemporary problems – social, political, psychological, philosophical. Blake brings to bear his wide reading and technical inventiveness on these works under a unified imaginative domain, viz. 'first the notion that man has a body distinct from his soul is to be expunged: this I shall do, by printing in the infernal method, by corrosives, which in Hell are salutary and medicinal, melting apparent surfaces away, and displaying the infinite which was hid.' And in *Jerusalem* Newton is reconciled to St. Paul's, the Gothic Cathedral of eternal truth takes everything into its structure.

Blake is one of those exalted in Lawrence's words:

> This is the beginning of all art, visual or literary or musical: be pure in spirit. It isn't the same as goodness. It is much more difficult and nearer the divine. The divine isn't only good, it is all things.

His eminence was possible by virtue of his ever transcendent way of life:

> My hands are labour'd day and night,
> And Ease comes never in my sight.
> My wife has no indulgence given
> Except what comes to her from heaven.
> We eat little, we drink less;
> This Earth breeds not our happiness.
> Another Sun feeds our life's streams …

Everything Blake did has its significance for us today. Some of his most pertinent prophecies are insufficiently understood in our time, and I hope I will be excused for referring one of his most vital calls to our immediately lethal prospect, the pressure of *elected* governments to the massacre of mankind:

> Rouze up, O Young Men of the New Age! set your foreheads against the ignorant Hirelings! For we have Hirelings in the Camp, the Court and the University, who would, if they could, for ever depress Mental and prolong Corporeal War. Painters! on you I call. Sculptors! Architects! Suffer not the fashionable Fools to depress your powers by the prices they pretend to give for contemptible works, or the expensive advertising boasts that they make of such works; believe Christ and His Apostles that there is a Class of Men whose whole delight is in Destroying.

Note

1 Editor: Horovitz's dating of the *Songs* and *Marriage* here does not accord with modern scholarly consensus.

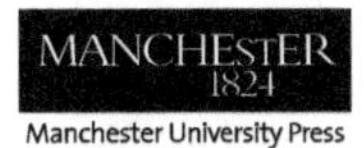
Manchester University Press

William Blake and (a Few of) His Friends in Our Time

MICHAEL HOROVITZ

Abstract

In this article, written in his signature style, Michael Horovitz reflects on his long-standing fascination with William Blake. He recalls how the spirit of Blake loomed large at the International Poetry Incarnation at the Albert Hall in the summer of 1965, where his fellow travellers, among them Adrian Mitchell, were driven by the nineteenth-century poet. Horovitz recounts the ways that Blake has continued to inform his artistic practices, which cut across from poetry to music and visual art.

Keywords: William Blake; International Poetry Incarnation; Vanessa Vie; poetry; jazz

A little while after I had published my 1957 piece on 'The Blake Renaissance' in *Oxford Opinion*, in celebration of his 200th birthday, I began to wonder what Great Grandfather William might feel about it himself.[1] It then occurred to me in a day-dream that he might find it a reasonably fair exposition, but with some misgiving about its primarily catering for British Academic Industries plc, in fine. Wherefore, might it not make more sense for me, nearing the threshold of leaving the University quite soon, to get on with something more like my own Renaissance?

So I founded *New Departures* publications, & also *Live New Departures* – an experimental arts circus which quite soon got enlarged to a series of internationalist *Jazz Poetry SuperJams* and *Poetry Olympics* festivals in order to bring artists & arts lovers of the world together, very much in the spirit of specific Blakean incentives – for example, his Jerusalemic aspiration that 'In my Exchanges every Land/Shall walk, & mine in every Land, / Mutual shall build Jerusalem: / Both heart in heart & hand in hand.'[2]

After the Beat & Protest 'Wholly Communion' Poetry Internationale which bade fair to levitate London's Royal Albert Hall in 1965, Ted Hughes affirmed something similar:

> The idea of global unity is not new, but the absolute necessity of it has only just arrived, like a sudden radical alteration of the sun, and we shall have to adapt or disappear. If the various nations are ever to make a working synthesis of their fierce contradictions, the plan of it and the temper of it will be created in spirit before it can be formulated or accepted in political fact. And it is in poetry that we can refresh our hope that such a unity is occupying people's imaginations everywhere, since poetry is the voice of spirit and imagination and all that is potential, as well as of the healing benevolence that used to be the privilege of the gods. It is not enough to say this once. It has to be said afresh year after year, in as many places and different languages as possible. And the effort of poets themselves to live up to their calling has to be renewed also, year after year.[3]

Bulletin of the John Rylands Library, Volume 98, No. 1 (Spring 2022), pp. 17–22, published by Manchester University Press.
http://dx.doi.org/10.7227/BJRL.98.1.3

Adrian Mitchell likewise spoke for many when he wrote and performed poems like his 'Lullaby for William Blake':

> Blakehead, babyhead,
> Your head is full of light.
> You sucked the sun like a gobstopper.
> Blakehead, babyhead,
> High as a satellite on sunflower seeds,
> First man-powered man to fly the Atlantic,
> Inventor of the poem which kills itself,
> The poem which gives birth to itself,
> The human form, jazz, Jerusalem
> And other luminous, luminous galaxies.
> You out-spat your enemies.
> You irradiated your friends.
> Always naked, you shaven, shaking tyger-lamb,
> Moon-man, moon-clown, moon-singer, moon-drinker,
> You never killed anyone.
> Blakehead, babyhead,
> Accept this mug of crude red wine –
> I love you.[4]

Our events and others broadly affiliated with them have gathered more and more momentum, bringing forward quite a number of then budding mega-talented heterodox and musical collaborators, including Paul McCartney, John Cooper Clarke, Patti Smith, Jeff Nuttall, Linton Kwesi Johnson, Joe Strummer, Paul Weller, Billy Bragg, Damon Albarn, Nick Cave and Ray Davies.

Davies's 'Waterloo Sunset' observes how the dirt-encrusted old Father Thames churns on, replete with a detritus of mega-chartered corrosions parallel to those Blake touches on in his eloquent poetic dirge for 'London', whose refrains admit of no redemption, no kind of 'safe and sound … paradise'.[5] A far cry from such conviction regarding anything like the near-mystical warmth relished by the KinkKing's lyrics, along with the tender-loving likes of his humbly representative couple, Terry & Julie. While 'Every Friday night' they '… cross over the river', the Blake speaker's downside experience of his native London grimly concludes: 'But most thro' midnight streets I hear / How the youthful Harlot's curse / Blasts the new born Infants tear, / And blights with plagues the Marriage hearse.'[6]

In *Children of Albion: Poetry of the Underground in Britain* (Penguin, 1969), I anthologised sixty-three more new troubadours, plus in 1992 yet another forty still younger *Grandchildren of Albion* (*New Departures* #17–20). And last year I published the debut volume by Vanessa Vie, *Open Windows, Open Doors*, as *New Departures* #42–43.[7] Her 'Ginger Cat in the Rain' (2013) affords a nice example of another intermedic & Blakean genre quite a lot of us have been developing over recent decades, namely '*Picture-Poetry*'.

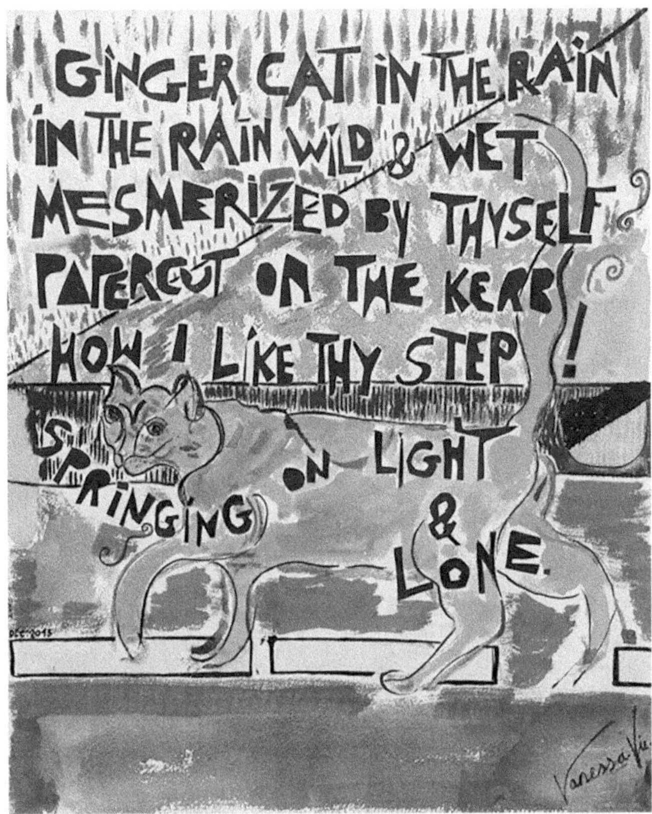

Figure 1 Vanessa Vie, *Ginger Cat in the Rain*, from the collection, *Open Windows, Open Doors* (New Departures, 2020). © Vanessa Vie.

I have continued with my own experiments in performance, poetry, pictures & songs, including Jazz Poems, Bebop Poems, Collage & Sound-Poems, oft-times accompanied by Vanessa, as well as by Pete Lemer's piano and Annie Whitehead's trombone, as the William Blake Klezmatrix band. In each genre, we tend to get all the happier when multiple echoes & extensions of Blake themes and impulses ensue – as suggested by titles like 'I am White, But O my Soul is Black', 'Forests of the Night', & 'Blake Was Right!'

A deluxe double LP box, *Jazz Poetry SuperJam* #1, complete with a lavishly documented & illustrated 30-page booklet focused on one of Pete Brown's & my earliest Jazz Poetry presentations, which surprised Southampton University in March 1962, features wondrous harmonies & improvisations by jazzers supreme Stan Tracey, Bobby Wellins, Jeff Clyne, John Mumford & Laurie Morgan at their sprightliest.[8]

As I am writing this appreciation of one of my most beloved and revered polymaths' polymaths, I hope I can be forgiven for adding a couple of celebratory tributes of my own: first a page combining the picture-poem 'For Chagall and my

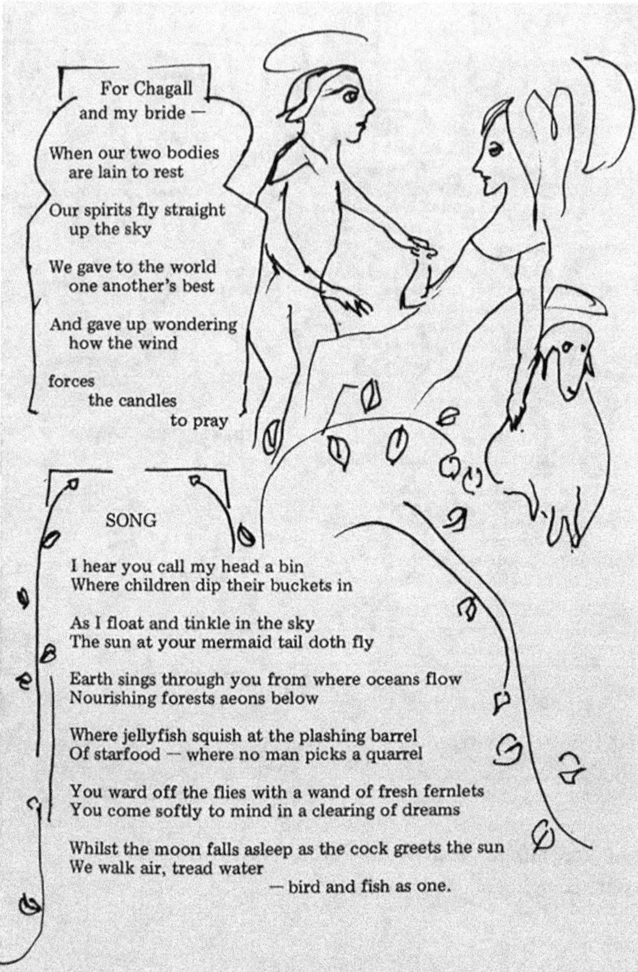

Figure 2 Michael Horovitz, *For Chagall and My Bride* and *Song*. © Michael Horovitz.

Bride' I wrote and drew in 1962, poised above the text of one of my Love Songs, as well as the above-mentioned painting, *Forests of the Night*.

In 1809 Blake presented the only substantial exhibition of his own works that took place in his lifetime, in the upstairs rooms of his brother's hosiery shop in Golden Square, Soho. *'Seen in My Visions': A Descriptive Catalogue of Pictures by William Blake* (Tate Publishing), is edited by Martin Myrone, curator of the display of what remains of the original exhibition, which was displayed at Tate Britain in 2009. The twenty colour reproductions, the artist's extensive comments on them, and Myrone's detailed notes all provide a poignant reminder of the degree to which Blake has too often remained a mountain too high to be seen plain by most of his peers.

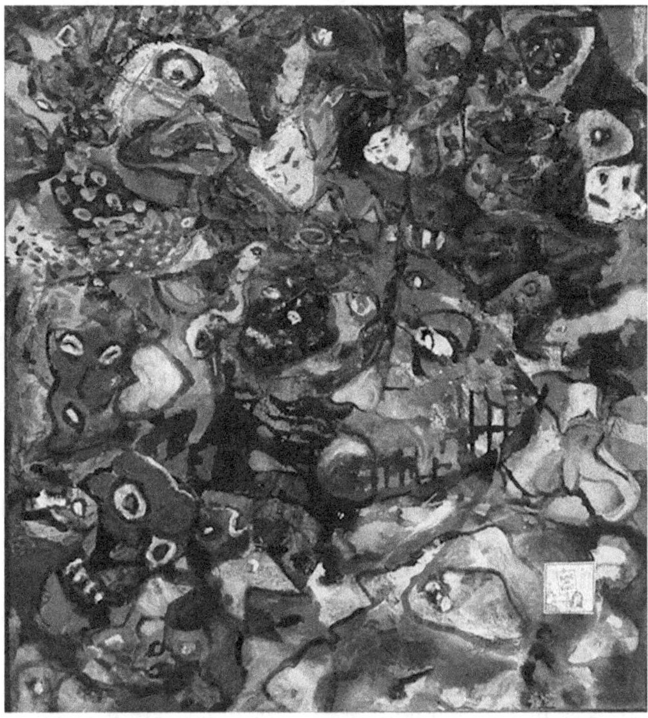

Figure 3 Michael Horovitz, *Forests of the Night*. © Michael Horovitz.

The only review the exhibition and the Catalogue received (from the pen of Robert Hunt, to his enduring shame) dismissed them in 1809 as 'a farrago of nonsense … the wild effusions of a distempered brain'.[9] But neither the strong-lined and brilliantly coloured lucidities of paintings such as 'Jacob's Ladder' and the depiction of Chaucer and his twenty-nine Canterbury pilgrims, nor the vigorous aperçus and unblinking challenges of the Catalogue, could conceivably be more delicately controlled yet revelatory.

And so dear reader, I urge you to (re)discover this uniquely dedicated genius's productions – via the handmade books that I recall making appointments lovingly to contemplate, when some were still available for public scrutiny in the Victoria & Albert Museum's National Art Library – & also via so many more available than ever to access, now that the majestic grandeur and profusion of his surviving verbal & non-verbal artworks & visions abound in countless reproductions & collections worldwide. If it is spiritual succour you wish for, seek deep in the heart of these monumentally divine Blakelands, and you will find it aplenty. In 'A Vision of the Last Judgment' (a manuscript addition to his *Catalogue*), Blake wrote:

> If the Spectator could enter into these Images in his Imagination, approaching them on the Fiery Chariot of his Contemplative Thought, if he could Enter into Noahs Rainbow or into his bosom or could make a Friend & Companion of one of these

> Images of wonder which always entreats him to leave mortal things (as he must know) then would he arise from his Grave, then would he meet the Lord in the Air & then he would be happy.[10]

Michael Horovitz, February–March 2021

Notes

1 'The Blake Renaissance' is reprinted as the previous article. It was first published in the student journal *Oxford Opinion* as part of its 'Special Art Issue', Hilary Term 1958.

2 D. Erdman, *The Complete Poetry and Prose of William Blake* (Berkeley: University of California Press, 1988), p. 173.

3 T. Hughes, 'Introduction to Poetry International 1967', cited in D. Weissbort, 'Ted Hughes and Truth', *Irish Pages*, 3 (2005), 187.

4 A. Mitchell, 'Lullaby for William Blake', in M. Horovitz (ed.), *Children of Albion: Poetry of the Underground in Britain* (Harmondsworth: Penguin, 1969), p. 219.

5 The Kinks, 'Waterloo Sunset' (1967).

6 *Ibid.*; Erdman, *The Complete Poetry and Prose of William Blake*, p. 27.

7 Vanessa grew up in northern Spain, but decided to stay in Albion for good after absorbing herself in the visual art and poetry of William Blake.

8 The album is still available from Gearbox Records.

9 Robert Hunt, 'Mr. Blake's Exhibition', *The Examiner* (17 September 1809), cited in G. E. Bentley, *The Stranger from Paradise: A Biography of William Blake* (New Haven and London: Yale University Press, 2001), p. 333.

10 Erdman, *The Complete Poetry and Prose of William Blake*, p. 560.

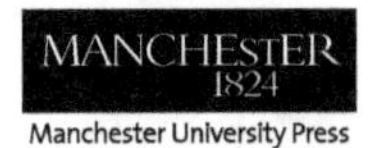

Manchester University Press

‘Invisible Gates Would Open’: W. B. Yeats and William Blake in the 1890s

JODIE MARLEY, THE UNIVERSITY OF NOTTINGHAM

Abstract
Yeats’s Blake criticism of the 1890s hinged on his knowledge of the esoteric and occult systems that he used as his framework for interpretation of the Romantic poet. This article examines *The Works of William Blake: Poetic, Symbolic, and Critical* (1893) and Yeats’s 1890s reviews of his contemporary Blake critics, as well as his relationship with the mystic poet and artist George William Russell (Æ), whom he repeatedly compared to Blake. Yeats’s emphasis on the importance of Boehme and Swedenborg in Blake’s system had a major influence on Blake’s critical legacy in the twentieth century, such as S. Foster Damon’s approach to Blake in *William Blake: His Philosophy and Symbols* (1924) and Kathleen Raine’s *Blake and Tradition* (1969). Yeats’s engagement with Blake in the 1890s also contributed to the popular conception of Blake as a mystic and visionary artist which still continues.

Keywords: William Blake; W. B. Yeats; George William Russell; Emanuel Swedenborg; mysticism; literary reception

In *The Trembling of the Veil* (1922), W. B. Yeats wrote, ‘I had an unshakeable conviction, arising how or whence I cannot tell, that invisible gates would open as they had opened for Blake, as they opened for Swedenborg, as they opened for Boehme, and that this philosophy would find its manuals of devotion in all imaginative literature.’[1]

Yeats’s statement concerns preparation for the Celtic Mystical Order he planned to create, with George Russell (pen name Æ) among its membership.[2] R. F. Foster cites Yeats’s reading in ‘Gaelic traditions’ and ‘myths and sagas researched in the National Library’ as the basis for the Order’s mythology.[3] Regarding its practices, Yeats describes these as a hybrid of Golden Dawn-influenced ritual work and group visionary experiences – the Hermetic Order of the Golden Dawn being an occult secret society of the late nineteenth and early twentieth centuries that counted Yeats among its most involved members.[4] However, the lines encapsulate Yeats’s lifelong attitude towards Blake. They express an admiration for the visionary faculty he saw in Blake’s life and works, while also placing Blake within the context of a greater ‘tradition’ of visionary writers, here the seventeenth-century spiritual alchemist Jacob Boehme, and the eighteenth-century Christian mystic Emanuel Swedenborg. Yeats’s description of the ‘unshakeable conviction’ that the gates would open ‘as they opened for Blake’ positioned him and his colleagues of the Celtic Mystical Order as the inheritors of Blake’s visionary legacy. Yet these lines from *The Trembling of the Veil* demonstrate the intersection of elements through which Yeats asserted his place as an inheritor of this visionary legacy. First, Blake’s name is not mentioned alone but alongside Boehme’s and Swedenborg’s, a common instance in Yeats’s writings on Blake. Second, the lines refer not to individual experience, but rather to Blake's influence on a wider community of creative people.

This article will first demonstrate Yeats's approach to Blake in the 1890s through the system outlined in his joint effort with Edwin J. Ellis, *The Works of William Blake: Poetic, Symbolic, and Critical* (1893), and through his reviews of other scholarship on Blake. Edward Larrissy and Deborah Dorfman both emphasise the significance of Yeats and Ellis's work to Blake's legacy in literary criticism.[5] Larrissy describes Yeats as 'one of the first serious scholars of Blake', and 'a pioneer in the promotion of Blake's excellence'.[6] Dorfman writes that the Yeats-Ellis collaboration, though containing what she describes as 'dubious mystical doctrine', ultimately helped 'sanction and provoke serious scholarship based on Blake's prophetic books'.[7] My article will not only delineate the critical impact Yeats's readings of Blake had within Blake studies, but the cultural impact that reading Blake as a 'mystic' had for later authors influenced by him. Second, I will examine Yeats's relationship with Russell and his responses to his literary output as well as his personal visionary experiences. This article's aim is to elucidate Blake's legacy through the work of Yeats and his circle, with the example of Russell as a case study of the kind of artists with whom he sought to grow closer. In his literary criticism of the 1890s, Yeats framed himself as an expert on mysticism in literature and thus as the only critic among his contemporaries who could truly 'understand' Blake. Yeats's background to his approach to Blake, and the legacy of his work on Blake's popular reception, was therefore coloured by both observations from his intellectual studies and from his personal experiences in friendships with visionaries.

In order to contextualise Yeats's approach to Blake and to see where Blake referenced the influences that the Irish poet emphasises so much, among them Swedenborg, Boehme and Paracelsus, some context is needed to track Yeats's reading habits and document a timeline of these references.

Yeats's fascination with Blake began in the early 1880s. This is when his biographer R. F. Foster dates Yeats's first encounters with Blake and Swedenborg, and it correlates with what Yeats writes in *The Trembling of the Veil*: that when he was 'fifteen or sixteen' his father gave him some of Blake's poetry to read.[8] Yeats was born in 1865 so, by his own account, he would have read Blake in 1880 or 1881. According to Foster, Yeats also read Swedenborg, who was 'first discovered by him in Dublin during the early 1880s' at a similar time, and reread Swedenborg almost a decade later when working on *The Works of William Blake*.[9] Yeats first met George William Russell – not yet using the pen name Æ – at art school in May 1884.[10] By that time, Yeats had read enough Swedenborg to be able to compare Russell to that eighteenth-century mystic: 'he [Russell] saw visions continually, perhaps more continually than any modern man since Swedenborg'.[11]

Yeats began *The Works of William Blake* in 1889, as we can surmise from his letter to Katherine Tynan on 8 March 1889: 'A friend [Ellis] is helping me, or perhaps I am helping him as he knows Blake much better than I do, or any one [*sic*] else perhaps.'[12] A note from Yeats to Lady Gregory, his dramatic collaborator, literary patron, fellow writer and friend, in her copy of the book, clarifies how much of *The*

Works of William Blake Yeats actually wrote or contributed to. It states that 'with the exception of the part called "The Symbolic System" almost all of the actual writing is by Ellis'.[13] 'The Symbolic System' is a delineation of the esoteric symbolism Yeats perceived within Blake's works, and its origins in previous spiritual philosophy. Throughout, he argued that knowing and understanding these influences on Blake was crucial to engagement with his work. The section constitutes just under half of the first volume, out of the three that comprised *The Works of William Blake*. Nevertheless, Yeats's work on 'The Symbolic System' would go on to irrevocably shape his readings of Blake, and his understanding of esoteric and spiritual philosophy.

Another significant factor in Yeats's approach to *The Works of William Blake* was his initiation into the Hermetic Order of the Golden Dawn, on 7 March 1890, one year into his Blake project.[14] Golden Dawn members were required to follow a set curriculum of esoteric studies to progress through the levels within the Order, which Mary K. Greer details as follows:

> The Golden Dawn emphasized scholarship and learning … The first four levels of initiation (Zealator to Philosophus) required primarily an intellectual development. Initiates memorised the Hebrew alphabet, the structure of the Kabbalistic Tree of Life, and astrological glyphs, terms and techniques.[15]

The Golden Dawn emphasised scholarship above all else as a means to advance within the Order. Many of the esoteric concepts learned by members were organised as systems, wherein each element had a multitude of meanings. To take the Kabbalistic Tree of Life as an example, each of the ten Sephiroth on the Tree corresponds to a different colour, astrological planet, stone, plant, perfume, and for several Sephiroth, a group of Tarot cards.[16] Through the Golden Dawn, Yeats grew familiar with esoteric ideas as expressed through set systems of correspondences, whether through Kabbalah or the astrological planets and houses. His early years of Golden Dawn membership corresponded with the four years he spent working on *The Works of William Blake*, 1889–93. Yeats's interpretation of Blake's body of work having a 'Symbolic System' came as much from his proclivity for working with esoteric systems in the Golden Dawn in his personal life as it did observing the mystic systems of correspondences in the works of Swedenborg, Boehme, and Paracelsus in his professional writing life. The unique convergence of these two different facets of his life created an idiosyncratic perspective on Blake equally informed by both his private and professional experiences.

Before embarking on an analysis of Yeats's Blake studies, it is important to note the specific connections to Boehme, Swedenborg and Paracelsus in Blake's life and work. We have documentary evidence of Blake's thoughts on Swedenborg and his attendance of a New Church conference through his annotations to Swedenborg and a register of that conference, but very little evidence in regard to Boehme and Paracelsus.[17] We cannot conclude from this, however, that Blake did *not* read Boehme or Paracelsus. These two authors, alongside Swedenborg, are mentioned by name in *The Marriage of Heaven and Hell* (1790): 'any man of mechanical talents may from the writings of Paracelsus or Jacob Behmen, produce ten thousand volumes of equal value with Swedenborg's'.[18]

In no correspondence, articles or autobiographical account does Yeats mention finding or accessing documentation or annotations proving specifically that Blake read Boehme, Paracelsus or Swedenborg. So rather than using an external source as evidence for Blake's engagement with these spiritual philosophers, Yeats's method of diving immediately into Swedenborg and Boehme studies in order to write on Blake was perhaps prompted by reading Blake's works themselves and noticing references and correspondences. When Yeats read Blake and Swedenborg in the early 1880s, he never mentions whether reading one author prompted reading the other, so we do not know whether he previously noticed the influence of Swedenborg on Blake in his teenage years. The three esoteric authors Yeats mentions most in his Blake writings – Boehme, Swedenborg and Paracelsus – are often mentioned together, as they are mentioned together in Blake's *Marriage*. In his scholarship on Blake, close analysis of the text was paramount, so the naming of these three esoteric authors in *Marriage* seems to be an important jumping-off point for Yeats's scholarship, one that would reverberate through the whole body of his writing on Blake. In his studies of the Romantic poet, Yeats proceeded by Blake's own example.

The Works of William Blake was published in 1893. Yeats's proposed contribution changed in structure over the four years he spent working on it. An early outline in a letter to Ellis in September 1890 presents a list of chapters which include: '12 Blake & Boehmen/13 Blake & Swedenborg/14 Blake & the Alchemists'.[19] Yeats's initial plan does not resemble the final structure of 'The Symbolic System'. In the three years that elapsed following this letter, Yeats abandoned the author-by-author chapter structure and instead wove references to Boehme, Swedenborg and Paracelsus throughout 'The Symbolic System', which comprises the third section (and almost half the total page count) of *The Works of William Blake*'s first volume. The weaving throughout of multiple esoteric references is in keeping with what he wrote to Ellis elsewhere in that letter, that 'My comparison of Blake Boehmen Alchemists Etc will not be confined to sepecial [*sic*] chapters but run through the general comment wherever it is useful as interpretation of Blake's meaning.'[20] Yeats structured his section of *The Works of William Blake* around an exploration of the esoteric symbolism he found in Blake's work. This idea of the symbol is one that he would further explore in his 1900 essay 'The Symbolism of Poetry', which he included in *Ideas of Good and Evil* (1903). Yeats's definition of symbolism in poetry there responds less to this specific Symbolist movement in literature than to his own understanding of the concepts of symbolism and correspondences within occultism and mysticism, where particular colours or symbols are believed to evoke, and invoke, specific spiritual phenomena. The lines 'all sounds, all colours, all forms, either because of their pre-ordained energies or because of long association, evoke indefinable and yet precise emotions, or, as I prefer to think, call down among us certain disembodied powers' exemplify this mode of thought.[21] To take an example from Yeats's own practice, Yeats describes the reaction of his friend William Sharp (who wrote as 'Fiona Macleod' and experienced her, almost spiritually, as a separate personality) to a Tattwa card in Paris in the 1890s.[22] Sharp experienced a vision of a funeral when visiting Yeats, who afterwards wrote:

> When he [Sharp] stood up to go he said, 'What is that?' pointing to a geometrical form painted upon a little piece of cardboard that lay upon my window sill. And then before I could answer, looked out of the window saying, 'There is a funeral passing.' I said, 'That is curious, as the Death symbol is painted upon the card'. I did not look, but I am sure there was no funeral.[23]

Yeats uses the example of Sharp's vision as evidence that symbols have the power to induce corresponding spiritual experiences, as Sharp's vision of a passing funeral corresponded with the Tattwa card's symbolising death.

In his analysis in 'The Symbolism of Poetry', Yeats applies the model of occult symbolism – where secret knowledge is hidden behind symbols or referenced indirectly using them – to literary criticism. In this, his approach is unique among Blake scholars. Not only does Yeats emphasise the significance of the mystic in Blake's work, but he engages with the theory of occult symbolism as his means and method of literary analysis. In this article, Yeats misquotes a single line of Blake's from *Europe a Prophecy* (1794): 'The gay fishes on the wave when the moon sucks up the dew' (where the line should read 'the gay fishes on the wave, when the cold moon drinks the dew').[24] He writes, 'take some line that is quite simple, that gets its beauty from its place in a story, and see how it flickers with the light of the many symbols that have given the story its beauty'.[25] That a single line of poetry could, for Yeats, reflect many symbols and many phenomena behind the apparent words on a page explains his approach in *The Works of William Blake.* It may be borne in mind should the reader become overwhelmed with the references to esoteric and spiritual systems Yeats includes on almost every page. The ideas he promotes in this 1900 essay had their origins in the way he read and perceived Blake in the 1880s and 1890s.

From the beginning of the project in 1889, Yeats wrote to his friends and acquaintances about his contribution to *The Works of William Blake* as one with a strong focus on mysticism and esoteric philosophy. He introduced the project to Katherine Tynan as 'a commentary on the mystical writing of Blake … for there is no clue printed anywhere to the mysterious "Prophetic Books" – [Algernon Charles] Swinburne and [Alexander] Gilchrist found them unintelligible'.[26] Here, Yeats not only frames 'The Symbolic System' as focused on the mystic elements of Blake, but also claims to be the first to do so. By doing so, Yeats positions himself not only as the literary critic, but also a seer of sorts, able to interpret messages within Blake's works that others might not initially see. Yeats would go on to present himself as such throughout his 1890s work on Blake, both during the composition of, and after, the publication of *The Works of William Blake*.

Another motivation for Yeats's approach was a defence of Blake's work and cultural legacy. By using his own reading into esoteric philosophy, Yeats sought to prove that Blake was not entirely 'unintelligible', but rather, that those who read his work, and like Gilchrist remained confused, simply needed more familiarity with Blake's spiritual frames of reference, whether from the Bible or Boehme, and would then understand his work.

Yeats describes his own experience working through this process to Ellis, writing that 'the reason I have not attacked Jerusalem & Milton is that the Biblical part, so important in both books, is still a blank to me, I am pushing on with Boehmen & Swedenborg reading, in the hope to find it clear up'.[27] Yeats writes here that he has a 'hope' that by reading Boehme and Swedenborg he might understand *Milton* and *Jerusalem*. The word 'hope' implies not a certainty but a certain faith in the act of reading Blake's esoteric influences: that if Yeats tried hard enough to read everything that influenced Blake, one day he too would understand what Blake's works meant.

As he advanced within the Golden Dawn – by the time of writing he had been a member for six months – the more he studied, so he expected that he would advance to a higher level of understanding of Blake's works. As he found links to Boehme and Swedenborg in Blake's works, he began to treat Blake's works as esoteric texts themselves. This attitude is reflected in another letter to Tynan in the early writing period, where he states 'the book must rouse a good deal of interest among literer[y] [*sic*] people & what will please me better influence for good the mystical societies through out [*sic*] Europe'.[28] Yeats's goal in including 'The Symbolic System' in *The Works of William Blake*, then, was twofold: to draw attention to Blake's esoteric influences in literary circles, and to recommend Blake's literary writing to mystics and occultists. Just two years before Yeats began his research on *The Works of William Blake*, George Russell may have been influenced to read some Blake in the summer of 1887 on Yeats' recommendation. However, according to Russell's biographer Henry Summerfield, 'he did not … penetrate deeply into the Prophetic Books other than *Thel* in spite of Yeats's enthusiastic talk about the Zoas'.[29] Nevertheless, Yeats trusted Russell's expertise enough to ask for his input on 'The Symbolic System'. Writing to Tynan, he observes, 'I notice by your letter that you see Russell now and then. Tell him to write to me – Tell him myself and a friend are writing a book on Blake and perhaps he will send me a letter with some Blake criticisms.'[30]

Yeats held other Blake critics to the same standards as himself in terms of their esoteric reading, both during and after work on *The Works of William Blake* finished. In March 1890, Yeats wrote to W. H. Dirks, the reader and adviser for the publisher Walter Scott, with a proposition for a new William Blake biography, which would be separate from *The Works of William Blake*. Yeats proposed himself as the ideal author for this biography, as

> Up to this their [*sic*] has not been a single fragment of writing on Blake by anyone who had the needful knowledge of traditional mysticism to understand his 'prophetic books' or even his smaller mystial [*sic*] poems or his more characteristic sayings and symbolical drawings. We have also at our command unpublished

> MSS of great value, including a poem full as I believe of the best poetry he has written.[31]

Yeats's argument that he had 'the needful knowledge of traditional mysticism' to write the book was of course one he would use again and again. In his letter to Dirks, however, he emphasises the 'unpublished MSS' that he and Ellis had access to, which was, in fact, *VALA*, or, *The Four Zoas*. Yeats mentioned this perhaps to draw interest to his proposed biography, which could, this letter suggests, incorporate previously unpublished material. Having access to an original Blake manuscript, albeit only through staying with John Linnell's family to copy it out, would also bolster the credibility of both his proposed project and his scholarly credentials.[32] The biography with Walter Scott evidently did not work out, as it is never mentioned again, but a few months later in August 1890, it was Ellis who secured the contract with publisher Bernard Quaritch who, according to Foster, 'agreed to publish their findings'.[33] Despite his claims of mystic knowledge and expertise in correspondence with friends and colleagues, Yeats received no payment from the publisher for his contribution to the book, and was only paid in copies of the book itself.[34]

It seems likely that the lack of formal recognition in the form of payment for his ideas from publishers Quaritch and Scott contributed to Yeats becoming more defensive than ever of his views regarding the importance of mysticism in Blake's work. Following the publication of *The Works of William Blake* in 1893, Yeats increasingly gestured towards his extensive readings of Boehme and Swedenborg as reason for his own intellectual authority on Blake's work. In his disparaging *Bookman* review of Richard Garnett's 1896 book *William Blake*, Yeats writes of Garnett:

> If the truth be told, Mr. Garnett, like Mr. Gilchrist, Mr. Rossetti, and almost every one [*sic*] who has ever written on the subject, does not show evidence of ever having given so much as a day's study to any part of Blake's mystical writing, or of having the knowledge necessary to make even prolonged study fruitful. This very book of 'Urizen' would alone convict commentators, for they have not even discovered the fact lying upon its threshold, that it is page by page a transformation, according to Blake's peculiar illumination, of the doctrines set forth in the opening chapters of the 'Mysterium Magnum' of Jacob Boehme.[35]

Although the review is of Garnett's work, he is not necessarily the main target of Yeats's criticism: Yeats blames earlier nineteenth-century Blake scholars like Gilchrist for encouraging what he perceives as an ignorance of the mystic aspect of Blake's work. Gilchrist and Garnett, however, were not necessarily ignorant of strains of mystic influence in Blake's work. Gilchrist describes Blake's *Songs of Experience* as 'more lucid writing than the books of prophecy last noticed – writing freer from mysticism and abstractions', and describes *Europe a Prophecy, The First Book of Urizen, The Song of Los* and *The Book of Ahania* as 'volumes of mystic verse'.[36] Garnett, thirty years later, actually names Blake's influences, describing them as 'the mystical writers he [Blake] did study, Boehme and Swedenborg', if only in order to then criticise Ellis's and Yeats's book.[37] Garnett writes:

> Messrs. Ellis and Yeats have devoted an entire volume of their three-volume work on Blake to the exposition of his visions. Their comment is often highly suggestive, but it is seldom convincing. When the right interpretation of a symbol has been found, it is usually self-evident. Not so with their explanations, which appear neither demonstrably wrong nor demonstrably right.[38]

It seems likely therefore that Yeats, in his own review of Garnett, was in a convoluted way attempting to defend his and Ellis's work in the face of criticism, while simultaneously demonstrating his intellectual familiarity with Blake by claiming one could not write on the poet without an understanding of his esoteric references.

Yeats's campaign to have the mysticism of Blake's work recognised in both a wider critical and cultural context began with an earlier review of a contemporary's Blake book in *Bookman*. In the review, this time on Laurence Housman's *Selections from the Writings of William Blake* (1893), Yeats, as in 1896, criticises previous scholars of Blake for misunderstanding his work and his legacy: 'Mr. Housman is less to blame than the tradition, and would be ashamed, if left to his own devices, to dismiss in a few patronising words books he has never pretended to understand, and probably never read more than a few lines of … I have done my best to put the tradition in the pillory, and would let him go free.'[39]

Although not an attack, his anger at previous scholars' treatment of Blake's mystic thought, and perhaps the negative reception of his and Ellis's book, is clearly perceptible in this review. However, his criticisms of Housman's book focused more on the editorial decisions in the presentation of Blake's poems.[40] Again, Yeats emphasises Blake's status as a mystic, and describes him as

> a great poet and a great painter, but he was a great mystic also, and cast his mysticism into a form which, however chaotic when compared with his lyrics and his painting, was in every way more beautiful than the form chosen by Swedenborg or Boehme. It was even less chaotic in many ways than the *Mysterium Magnum* and *Aurora*.[41]

Here, not only is Blake positioned as an inheritor of the mystic tradition of Swedenborg and Boehme, but his work is presented by Yeats as a progression, a refinement, of Boehme's and Swedenborg's ideas. The dynamic of Blake's spiritual influence, for Yeats, therefore works in two ways. Blake's writings are not only influenced by Boehme and Swedenborg, but help the esoterically inclined reader understand older works through the esoteric symbolism Yeats highlights in Blake. The 'form' of his work is not only 'less chaotic', implying that Yeats saw a distillation of philosophy or a stricter system on Blake's part in comparison to his forebears, but also that his manner of presenting ideas was more 'beautiful', implying Yeats saw an aesthetic beauty there that he believed Boehme's and Swedenborg's works did not possess. We can link this perception of Yeats's, that Blake's being an artist benefited the expression of mystic ideas, to his own circle of friends and acquaintances. To name several examples, Moina Mathers was a painter, Russell was a painter and writer, Fiona Macleod and William Sharp were writers, Florence Farr was a writer and actor, and Pamela Colman Smith was a painter, writer and occasional performance artist. For Yeats, their involvement with one of these activities strengthened and brought nuance to the other. Yeats, as both poet and occultist, saw esoteric references in Blake's work and believed himself the ideal person to contribute to Blake's legacy on both critical and literary levels, as well as to follow what he saw as the mystic tradition present in Blakes work.

In 'The Symbolic System', Yeats mentions Swedenborg, Boehme and Paracelsus, in passing, many times. The significance of Yeats's constant comparisons of Blake to Swedenborg and Boehme is that Yeats's entire 'Symbolic System' hinges on superimposing these two figures in particular over Blake's own system. I have chosen to demonstrate this by an analysis of the first two chapters of Yeats's 'Symbolic System'. These chapters are more straightforward to read as they serve as an introduction of sorts to Yeats's often dense approach, useful for my purposes of exemplifying how Yeats's methods of analysis function.

In the first chapter, 'I. The Necessity of Symbolism', Yeats aligns the concept of Blake's opposites and the poetic genius with Swedenborg's concept of the 'discrete degrees'.[42] Yeats uses the example of good and evil in Blake's *The Marriage of Heaven and Hell* as opposites, so that each opposite, plus the poetic genius, makes three discrete degrees according to Swedenborg's system. According to Swedenborg, there are two kinds of degrees, called 'continuous' and 'discrete'. The scale of continuous degrees is likened to 'the degrees of light decreasing on to obscurity', whereas discrete degrees are differentiated from continuous degrees 'as cause from effect, and as what produces from production'.[43] Although the imagery and concepts Swedenborg uses to describe these degrees are very different, both sets of degrees have in common the quality of ordering the universe: that in this system, 'one thing proceeds from another, and that from a third, and so on … he that has no perception of these degrees of order, can have no idea of the distinction of the heavens'.[44]

The system of degrees in Swedenborg's system is a development of his theory of the correspondences: namely that everything on earth corresponds to something in the heavens, as discussed in *A Treatise Concerning Heaven and Hell* (1778). Yeats's choice of aligning Blake with this system of degrees immediately structures the world in Blake's works into something much larger than itself. Yeats writes that 'discrete degrees are related to each other by "correspondence" and by that alone, for all other methods imply identity'.[45] After discussing Blake's 1788 annotations to *The Divine Love and Wisdom* (1763), in which Blake objects to, and corrects, Swedenborg's theory of the degrees, Yeats continues: '"Is it not evident," he [Blake] writes, "that one degree will not open the other." He is combatting a statement of Swedenborg's that a child is born in the merely "natural degree," and that he passes from that to the others.'[46] Thus, when Yeats aligns Blake's system of opposites and the poetic genius with Swedenborg's degrees, he incorporates the above commentary of Blake's in his reading of Swedenborg, describing the opposites and the poetic genius as being in a relationship where they proceed out of each other.

Yeats's conception of a system of opposites and the poetic genius being in a mutually generative relationship also replicates the dynamic of separate elements in Boehme's system. For Boehme, both in *The Three Principles* (1619) and his seven properties or qualities as outlined in *The Aurora* (1612), each principle or quality is born out of those that preceded it. In the case of Boehme's three principles, the system which most closely recalls Yeats's conclusions in his 'Chapter I', Boehme writes, 'thus there is one being and not two, but two properties, whereof one is not the other, nor eternally can become so. As the spirit's property cannot be fire and light, and yet proceeds from fire out of light, and could not subsist either from fire or from light alone.'[47] Yeats's structure of the chapter, and how he discusses Blake's influences, reflects the structure of both Swedenborg's system of discrete degrees and Boehme's systems of principles and qualities. Blake's esoteric influences, for Yeats, must be considered holistically: as proceeding out of each other. Yeats does not discuss Boehme in depth until Chapter II, after his first discussion of Swedenborg's degrees. His introduction to Boehme-in-Blake explains the concept of the looking-glass, wherein God sees 'Himself as the Son, His love for His own unity, His self-consciousness, and enters on that eternal meditation about Himself which is called the Holy Spirit.'[48]

Again, the image Yeats selects here, introducing the ways Blake's and Boehme's systems intersect, is an image of the reflection of one concept in and by another. This is essential to understanding Yeats's interpretations of Blake and the influence this had on Blake's reception afterwards, both critically and culturally: that Blake represents a larger visionary heritage that came before him and remains reflected in a wider visionary legacy after his death. This phenomenon echoes throughout Yeats's critical work on Blake, whether through seeing Blake's system in Swedenborg's degrees in *The Works of William Blake*, or as in his later review of Garnett, where he claimed to see Boehme's *Mysterium Magnum* outlined in *The First Book of Urizen*.[49] Unlike Yeats's circle of friends and acquaintances, Blake, Boehme and Swedenborg never met. Yet Yeats identified, through literary reception, an active dialogue between the ideas of the dead and his living contemporaries, which eternally passed through each of their works and built up, as the works were read again and again by new audiences. Yeats believed himself and his circle of friends, including George Russell, to be receptors of that dialogue started by Blake.

Yeats met George Russell at art school in 1884, and their relationship from then until the late 1880s seems to have been very close.[50] Russell certainly made an impression on Yeats during this time, and is described in Yeats's autobiographical writings primarily as a man who saw visions. The connection to Blake was made from very early on. Tynan wrote in her diary in 1887, 'W. Y. brought a boy, George Russell, with him. Fond of mysticism, and extraordinarily interesting. Another William Blake!'[51] The current continued into Yeats's later autobiographical writings. For example, in *Reveries Over Childhood and Youth* (1916), Russell is described as 'George Russel [*sic*], "Æ," the poet, and mystic. He did not paint the model as we tried to, for some other images rose always before his eyes … and already he spoke to us of his visions.'[52] In *The Trembling of the Veil*, describing the events of a few years later, Russell is presented as a Dublin mystic associated with the Theosophical lodge at Ely Place; 'men watched him with awe or with bewilderment; it was known that he saw visions continually, perhaps more continually than any modern man since Swedenborg'.[53]

Yet the aspect of the dreamy seer in Russell's character as Yeats perceived it found another outlet in Yeats's 1891 article 'An Irish Visionary'. Yeats wrote, 'the poetry he recited me was full of his nature and his visions', and then described a vision of Russell's as it occurred while they are both in the room: 'suddenly it seemed to me that he was peering about him a little eagerly. "Do you see anything, X – ?" I said. "A shining, winged woman, covered by her long hair, is standing by the doorway," he answered'.[54] This account is striking in its similarity to accounts of Blake's visions in biographies and in popular culture and represents an early example in Blake's cultural afterlife – that is, in the nineteenth century, still within the century of his death – of a later artist and poet being compared to the 'visionary' Blake.[55]

Yeats's memories of Russell from the mid-1880s to the early 1890s are crucial for how he writes about Russell and how Yeats, at first hand, perceived mystic experience in one of his close friends. There are similarities between how Russell's speech is described and how Blake's 'unintelligibility' is described by the critics Yeats wrote about so viciously in his reviews of the 1890s: at art school, 'his conversation, so lucid and vehement to-day, was all but incomprehensible'.[56] Russell's eerie similarity to Blake in these examples posits him, in Yeats's autobiographical and critical writing, as an ideal inheritor of Blake's visionary legacy. Their 1880s friendship was a formative time for them both, despite their eventual divergences of spiritual beliefs: Russell became far more deeply involved in Theosophy after Yeats left for the Golden Dawn. It was during the 1880s that both of them began their reading on esoteric and occult themes, which would prove lifelong influences on their works. We know from Yeats that he read Blake and Swedenborg prior to meeting Russell, but as noted previously, Yeats's attempts to encourage his friend to read Blake in 1887 were only partially successful. However, that same year, Russell was also reading Boehme, two years before and independently of Yeats.[57] Russell, therefore, was not only a visionary to Yeats, but an artist versed in esoteric thought – at the time more well-read in Boehme, one of Blake's influences, than Yeats himself. Although never a Golden Dawn member, he had strong ties to the Dublin Theosophists, and possessed exactly the kind of visionary capabilities Yeats was looking for to contribute to his Order. He was exactly the kind of artist Yeats envisioned taking on Blake's legacy.

Yeats's literary criticism of the 1890s and his friendships with mystically inclined artists acted in a mutually beneficial way. In defining possible esoteric and mystic sources for writings that other Blake critics found 'unintelligible', Yeats was legitimising a wider body of Blake's work in the eyes of nineteenth-century critics: Blake's visions had historical and theological precedents. Although his work was poorly received by critics like Garnett, Yeats managed to disperse and promote Blake among his friends and contemporaries, convincing Russell to read Blake, later advising and collaborating with Pamela Colman Smith on an edition of Blake's poetry for her Green Sheaf Press (never published), and expressing the hope to Tynan that Blake would be picked up by mystics specifically.[58] The relationship also helped to legitimise the works of his friends by placing them in a specific cultural legacy of writers and artists whose work was inspired by visionary experience.

To conclude, the critical legacy of Yeats's *Works of William Blake* survives as scholars continue to explore Blake's spiritual influences. This does not necessarily mean that these critics work as Yeats did, overlaying system upon complicated system. Rather, by emphasising the influence of Swedenborg and Boehme, Yeats drew attention to these influences of Blake's and allowed critical conversation to continue into the following centuries. In particular, Yeats's influence on critical Blake studies can be found in those works by authors whose work considers Blake's influences holistically, that is, considering the ways each influence interacts with another to form a larger, Blakean framework. Diverse examples of this kind of criticism include S. Foster Damon's *William Blake: His Philosophy and Symbols* and Kathleen Raine's *Blake and Tradition*, in addition to Edward Larrissy's *William Blake* and the first chapters of Kevin Fischer's *Converse in the Spirit: William Blake, Jacob Boehme, and the Creative Spirit*.[59]

Furthermore, we may examine the influence that Yeats's concept of a 'mystic' Blake, and the canonical legitimacy Blake's mysticism gave to Yeats's artistic circle, has had on popular culture more generally. A well-known mid-twentieth-century example of Blake's visionary reception is the Beat poet Allen Ginsberg, who experienced and wrote about a 1948 vision of Blake, 'during which he heard Blake's disembodied voice and experienced a simultaneous expansion of consciousness that both prefigured and stimulated his later interest in psychedelics'.[60] Here, Ginsberg not only experienced a vision like his predecessor Blake, but actually received a vision *of* Blake, so the phenomenon equally contributes to both Blake's reception as a poet who experienced visions and his relevance towards those whose artistic work centres around visionary experience.

The influence I describe remains intrinsic to Blake's cultural reception to this day, in the first quarter of the twenty-first century. In the Afterword to the most recent Blake retrospective exhibition at Tate Britain, Alan Moore chooses to describe Blake's visions of the Ghost of a Flea and the Ancient of Days in his essay, out of all the biographical material available.[61] Although he describes a kind of communal psychic influence in the air of eighteenth-century Lambeth, 'visions buried in its stones and mortar waiting for their revelation', the final impression of Blake for the reader is one of an isolated artist who saw spirits and visions.[62] It is still very much in keeping with the late nineteenth-century views of Yeats, Gilchrist and Garnett, demonstrating an ongoing influence of these perspectives of Blake as an artist who saw visions. Although Yeats, Gilchrist and Garnett all highlighted the 'mystical' nature of Blake's work, only Yeats explored Blake's influences with the intention of clarifying Blake's work and bringing a greater cultural appreciation of his esoteric ideas to the fore. His Blake differed from Gilchrist's and Garnett's. Yes, Yeats's Blake was a mystic as Gilchrist and Garnett also perceived him, but from Yeats's perspective, his work was accessible if readers approached it with a mind that was open to older spiritual philosophies and visionary history.

In an article by Kae Tempest, a poet, spoken word artist and the current president of the William Blake Society, the ideas of visionary influence, inheritance and communion come together in full force. Tempest explains the correlation between their own visionary experiences and Blake's: 'I had also seen angels in Peckham Rye, and each time I passed that tree where he had seen his, I was struck by the weight of it. He left a living cast of spirits that populated the very place I lived.'[63] Blake's visions find sympathy in Tempest's own lived experience. In the context of the article, Tempest describes their feelings of connectedness to Blake through their work's initially being misunderstood through their early career.[64] Blake's visionary abilities, and his belief in them, as Tempest describes create firstly a sense of reassurance that others with similar visions came before them. Tempest then emphasises that both comfort and inspiration can be found in being part of Blake's visionary legacy: their experience correlates with what Yeats saw in his friend Russell. Blake and Tempest are both isolated in their account, but find communion and connection that breaches the laws of time and space, fuelled by their conception of visionary experience.

Swedenborg's and Boehme's influence came to Blake when they were dead, as did his vision of Boehme and Paracelsus. Blake when dead came to Yeats, to Russell, to Ginsberg; and comes to Moore, to Tempest. The idea of a visionary literary reception, wherein Blake's successors experience his literary influence via visionary and spiritual means as well as through more conventional written forms, determines that these authors live on across time, in spirit, through the work of others. Authors die, but their inspiration is eternal.

Notes

1 W. B. Yeats, *The Trembling of the Veil* (London: T Werner Laurie Ltd, 1922), p. 136.

2 R. F. Foster, *W. B. Yeats: A Life, Volume I: The Apprentice Mage* (Oxford: Oxford University Press, 1997), p. 180.

3 *Ibid.*, p. 196.

4 Yeats, *The Trembling of the Veil*, pp. 140–3 (p. 137).

5 W. B. Yeats and Edwin J. Ellis, *The Works of William Blake: Poetic, Symbolic, and Critical, Volume I* (London: Bernard Quaritch, 1893).

6 Edward Larrissy, *Blake and Modern Literature* (Houndmills: Palgrave Macmillan, 2006), p. 37; Larrissy, 'Blake, Eliot and Auden', in Sarah Haggarty (ed.), *William Blake in Context* (Cambridge: Cambridge University Press, 2019), p. 219.

7 Deborah Dorfman, *Blake in the Nineteenth Century: His Reputation as a Poet From Gilchrist to Yeats* (London: Yale University Press, 1969) pp. 192, 226.

8 Foster, *W. B. Yeats: A Life, Volume I*, p. 99; Yeats, *The Trembling of the Veil*, p. 5.
9 *Ibid.*
10 P. Kuch, *Yeats and A.E., 'The Antagonism That Unites Dear Friends'* (Gerrards Cross: Colin Smythe, 1986), p. 1.
11 Yeats, *The Trembling of The Veil*, p. 124.
12 Yeats, letter to Katherine Tynan dated 8 March 1889, in *Collected Letters, Volume One*, ed. John Kelley and Eric Domville (Oxford: Oxford University Press, 1986), p. 151.
13 Kelley and Domville (eds), *Collected Letters, Volume One*, p. 226, n. 4.
14 *Ibid.*, p. xiv.
15 Mary K. Greer, *Women of the Golden Dawn: Rebels and Priestesses* (Rochester: Park Street Press, 1995), p. 58.
16 A full list of Sephiroth correspondences can be found in Israel Regardie, 'Chapter Three', *A Garden of Pomegranates* (Saint Paul: Llewellyn Publications, 1970), pp. 37–64.
17 G. E. Bentley Jr, *Blake Records* (Oxford: Oxford University Press, 1969), p. 35.
18 William Blake, *The Marriage of Heaven and Hell* (1790), in David V. Erdman (ed.), *The Complete Poetry and Prose of William Blake* (New York: Anchor Books, 1988), p. 43, plate 21.
19 Yeats, letter to Edwin J. Ellis, dated '[? 6 September 1890]' in *Collected Letters, Volume One*, p. 224. Yeats had an idiosyncratic habit of spelling Boehme as 'Boehmen', which combines the original German spelling with the traditional English variant 'Behmen'. On the date, editor John Kelly writes that in general, 'Yeats rarely dated his letters in full, many of these dates, the most accurate we have been able to fix upon, are conjectural and appear within square brackets, often with a preceding query', p. xxvii.
20 *Collected Letters, Volume One*, p. 227.
21 Yeats, 'The Symbolism of Poetry', in *Ideas of Good and Evil, The Collected Works in Verse and Prose of William Butler Yeats, Vol. 6* (London: Chapman & Hall Limited, 1908), p. 190.
22 William F. Halloran specifies that it was a Tattwa card Yeats used in this anecdote, and suggests that Yeats used the card specifically to induce a vision for Sharp in Halloran, 'W. B. Yeats, William Sharp, and Fiona Macleod: A Celtic Drama, 1897', in *Yeats Annual No. 14: Yeats and the Nineties* (Houndmills: Palgrave, 2001), p. 166.
23 Yeats, *The Trembling of the Veil*, p. 214.
24 Yeats, 'The Symbolism of Poetry', p. 189; Blake, *Europe a Prophecy* (1794) in *The Complete Poetry and Prose*, p. 65, plate 14, line 3.
25 Yeats, 'The Symbolism of Poetry', p. 190.
26 Yeats, letter to Katherine Tynan dated 8 March [1889] in *Collected Letters, Volume One*, p. 151.
27 Yeats, letter to Ellis dated [?] 6 September 1890, *Collected Letters, Volume One*, p. 224.
28 Yeats, letter to Tynan dated *c.*18 May 1890, *Collected Letters, Volume One*, p. 218.
29 H. Summerfield, *That Myriad Minded Man: A Biography of George William Russell "A. E." 1867–1935* (Gerrards Cross: Colin Smythe Ltd, 1975), p. 26.
30 Yeats, letter to Tynan, dated 21 March [1889] in *Collected Letters, Volume One*, p. 156.
31 Yeats, letter to W. H. Dirks, dated 15 March [1890] in *Collected Letters, Volume One*, p. 213.

32 Foster, *W. B. Yeats: A Life, Volume I*, p. 100.
33 *Ibid.*
34 *Ibid.*
35 Yeats, Review (from *Bookman*, April 1896) of Richard Garnett's *William Blake* (London, 1896) in *Uncollected Prose by W. B. Yeats, Volume I*, ed. John P. Frayne (London: Macmillan, 1970), p. 402.
36 Alexander Gilchrist, *The Life of William Blake* (1863), ed. Ruthven Todd (London: J. M. Dent & Sons, 1982), pp. 100, 106.
37 R. Garnett, *William Blake: Painter and Poet* (London: Seely and Co. Limited, 1895), p. 32.
38 *Ibid.*
39 Yeats, Review (from *Bookman*, August 1893) of Laurence Housman's *Selections from the Writings of William Blake* (1893), *Uncollected Prose by W. B. Yeats, Volume I*, p. 283.
40 Yeats, *Bookman* review of Housman, p. 281.
41 *Ibid.*, pp. 282–3.
42 Yeats and Ellis, *The Works of William Blake, Volume I*, pp. 238–41.
43 Emanuel Swedenborg, *A Treatise Concerning Heaven and Hell, containing a relation of many wonderful things therein, as heard and seen by the author* (London: J. Phillips [etc.], 1778), p. 24.
44 *Ibid.*
45 Yeats and Ellis, *The Works of William Blake, Volume I*, p. 237.
46 *Ibid.*
47 Jacob Boehme, *Six Theosophic Points* (1620), trans. John Rolleston Earle (Michigan: University of Michigan Press, 1970), p. 26.
48 Yeats and Ellis, *Works of William Blake, Volume I*, p. 247.
49 Yeats, Review of Richard Garnett's *William Blake* (London, 1896), in *Uncollected Prose*, p. 402.
50 Kuch, *Yeats and A.E.*, p. 1; Yeats, *The Trembling of The Veil*, p. 127.
51 Tynan, quoted in John Eglinton, *A Memoir of AE George William Russell* (London: Macmillan & Co., 1937), p. 14.
52 Yeats, *Reveries Over Childhood and Youth* (New York: The Macmillan Company, 1916), pp. 93–4.
53 Yeats, *The Trembling of the Veil*, p. 124.
54 W. B. Yeats, 'An Irish Visionary' (first published October 1891 in the *National Observer*), in *Writings on Irish Folklore, Legend and Myth*, ed. Robert Welch (London: Penguin, 1993), pp. 73, 74.
55 See, for example, the depiction of William Blake's vision of the Ghost of a Flea in Alan Moore and Eddie Campbell's *From Hell* (1989) (London: Knockabout, 2006), Chapter 14, pp. 9–10, 16–17; and Gilchrist's account of the creation of 'The Visionary Heads', in *The Life of William Blake*, pp. 263–4.
56 Yeats, *Reveries Over Childhood and Youth*, p. 94.
57 *Ibid.*, p. 22; Foster, *W. B. Yeats: A Life, Volume I*, p. 99.

58 Summerfield, *That Myriad Minded Man*, p. 26; Elizabeth Foley O'Connor, *Pamela Colman Smith: The Untold Story* (Stamford: U.S. Games Systems, Inc., 2018), p. 56; Yeats, letter to Tynan dated *c.*18 May 1890, *Collected Letters, Volume One*, p. 218.

59 S. Foster Damon, *William Blake: His Philosophy and Symbols* (London: Constable and Company, 1924); Kathleen Raine, *Blake and Tradition* (London: Routledge & Kegan Paul, 1969); Edward Larrissy, *William Blake* (Oxford: Basil Blackwell, 1985); Kevin Fischer, *Converse in the Spirit: William Blake, Jacob Boehme, and the Creative Spirit* (Madison: Fairleigh Dickinson University Press, 2004).

60 Luke Walker, 'Allen Ginsberg's Blakean Albion', *Comparative American Studies: An International Journal*, 11:3 (2013), p. 228, doi: 10.1179/1477570013Z.00000000043.

61 Alan Moore, 'Afterword', in Martin Myrone and Amy Concannon, *William Blake* (London: Tate Publishing, 2019), p. 200.

62 *Ibid.*, p. 199.

63 Kae Tempest, 'Blakean Intensity', in *VALA: The Journal of the Blake Society*, 1 (2020), p. 4: www.blakesociety.org/VALA-Issue-1.pdf.

64 *Ibid.*, p. 5.

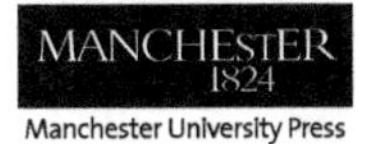

Manchester University Press

William Blake and the Spiritual Forms of Citizenship and Hospitality

COLIN TRODD, UNIVERSITY OF MANCHESTER

Abstract

The first part of this article focuses on previously unstudied materials relating to the critical recuperation of William Blake in the period between *c*.1910 and 1930. It notes how commentators utilised ideas of citizenship and hospitality when they attempted to modernise Blake's interests and concerns. It explains how these distinctive critical idioms were constructed, what they had in common and how they situated Blake in larger public arguments about the social significance of cultural creativity. The second part of the article traces the ramifications of this new way of thinking about Blake by noting his appearance in modernist and neo-romantic art criticism in the 1930s and 1940s.

Keywords: aesthetics; citizenship; community; hospitality; imagination; liberty; romantic; vision

On 6 September 1940 it was reported that Winston Churchill, in preparation for imminent invasion, had put himself in the position of Adolf Hitler attacking the British Isles.[1] On the same day, the cultural commentator Paul Bloomfield delivered a paper to fellow members of The Royal Society of Arts, London, entitled 'William Blake and his Albion'. The following week, the British High Command agreed that the long-anticipated invasion was about to begin.[2] It can be inferred that the thinking behind these important disclosures may have coloured Bloomfield's idiosyncratic belief that the spiritual form of William Blake possessed greater firepower than the entire Nazi war machine. Whatever the case, Bloomfield, a level-headed and clubbable member of the literary establishment, who contributed to *The Listener* and *The Manchester Guardian*, was not inclined to offer polite comments on Blake's art; instead, his titanic Blake, endowed with the revolutionary power of transfiguration, presided over a celestial ecclesia with the intention of indicting 'the forces that have been let loose against Jerusalem'. Bloomfield's vatic subject was motivated by the conviction that 'the significance of human history is moral', and that the real purpose of art is to 'testify to the dignity of mankind'. Seen from this angle, Blake, a compelling combination of Hegelian World Spirit and Ruskinian prophet, acted as 'agent of spiritual power' and 'apocalyptic vibration'. He was, we are forced to surmise, re-radiating the principle of liberty by generating a humanised vision of the universe.[3]

Versions of this convoluted, shape-shifting argument – in which Blake's immersion in the eschatological dramas pictured in his own designs could be traced to a desire to produce abiding symbols of citizenship – were made by other cultural commentators for whom Blake seemed to be the answer to another important matter: was it possible for the modern artist to create individual critical works

Bulletin of the John Rylands Library, Volume 98, No. 1 (Spring 2022), pp. 39–53, published by Manchester University Press.
http://dx.doi.org/10.7227/BJRL.98.1.5

which combined cognitive mastery of aesthetic form with moral integrity of aesthetic experience?[4] As I will illustrate, these conceptions, where the value of Blake's composite art is at once political and ontological, generated two overlapping formulations of his cultural identity.[5] The first was the belief that Blake generated an expressive art arising from the performance of visionary perception as manifestation of utopian hope. The second was the belief that he generated an expressive art arising from the performance of visionary perception as belief in the ultimate economy of the universe. These large explanatory arrangements give force to Bloomfield's account of Blake's aesthetic, where his artistic creativity is taken to confirm the meta-historical claims of citizenship as a source of human wisdom and a sign of human destiny.

This utopic strand of criticism, in which the goal of art is to offer a picture of future possibilities, was a reaction to the earlier modelling of Blake proffered by A. C. Swinburne and Arthur Symons, for whom Blake's restless and crowded designs constituted an inflection point in the history of aesthetics. As they saw it, Blake's composite art was the representation of the dynamic relationship between internality and externality; it was a condition of creative aesthetic life where experience was experiencing itself.[6] In contrast, Bloomfield's Blake, no less outlandish, was an imperious analyst of modern existence and represented collective, progressive self-determination. This point matters enormously for our sense of the material conditions under which Bloomfield produced his reading of the peculiar power of Blake's vision. From Bloomfield's vantage point, at the beginning of the Battle of Britain, it was because Blake's art was forever taking place on the surface of modern life that he could be co-opted to fight the Nazis on the ethical–spiritual plane. Note too that Bloomfield's reading, in which Blakean culture is put at the centre of collective national memory, turned Blake into a one-person spiritual Witenagemot. This striking attitude, where Blake as 'citizen of Jerusalem' signified the capacity to reimagine the nation in political argument, was well entrenched in British cultural criticism.[7] Benjamin Kirkman Gray, an economic historian who specialised in the history of philanthropy, prefigured this line of thought in a fascinating but overlooked account of the character of Blake's art.

Unlike Bloomfield, Kirkman Gray was not a member of the metropolitan cultural elite, nor did he belong to the academic establishment.[8] These arrangements may explain his distinctive account of the social conditions of modernity, in which Blake appears as a forward-thinking subject opposed to utilitarian accounts of social being. 'The Mind of a Londoner' (1910) deploys a critical lexicon derived from John Ruskin's social and political writings, where the modern artist is compelled to detach the idea of human wealth from any theory of economic performance. From Kirkman Gray's position, Blake's productions reflect on the 'social nature of man', address 'the conditions of a healthy political life', and thus adjudicate in the battle between cooperation and competition. Like Bloomfield, Kirkman Gray alights on *Jerusalem* (1804–20), which he calls 'an essay on citizenship, citizenship properly understood being an episode in the drama of the unfolding of human power'. Part of his reasoning here was the creation of the fabulously far-fetched proposal that

Jerusalem 'is not by any means an elementary handbook for administrators, but the reading of it might, with advantage, be imposed on all mayors and Parliament-men, since it is their business to discuss the means by which this development of human power may be furthered and aided'.[9]

As one would expect, neither mayors, Members of Parliament nor representatives of a modern Witenagemot rushed forward to declare that Blake's most mysterious and opaque production was an irresistible component in the construction of humanitarian reform programmes.[10] Nonetheless, Kirkman Gray predicted the emergence of what should be called a Ruskin-inspired strand of cultural criticism by arguing that Blake was an agent of popular sovereignty rather than the elliptical stranger-god found in those early twentieth-century writings which were influenced by E. J. Ellis and W. B. Yeats, both of whom set out to demonstrate how Blake produced his own systematic metaphysics.[11] More than this, by claiming a relationship between individual liberty and social development, Kirkman Gray connected Blake to the conceptual apparatus of Ruskinian ethical socialism, which proposed that the purpose of imaginative culture was the provision of moral-practical insights for the workings of the social world. In other words, Kirkman Gray's normative Blake predicted the interests of the Fabian Society by formulating a holistic aesthetic shaped by ideas of social renewal and active citizenship.

Kirkman Gray insisted that as Blake's true subject was the moral activity of society, so his art was a practical response to the social world. However odd it seemed when Blake expressed it in graphic or literary terms, his model of the imagination was shaped by the realities of everyday life. Blake's project was the creation of aesthetic forms that enacted participation in social and political spheres, a radical materialism modelled on the idea that civil association was an expression of liberty. This mixture of rationalist and utopian thought was incorporated into *Jerusalem*, which Kirkman Grey regarded as an attempt to produce a mythographic cartography where districts of London are mental states. From whatever angle he looked at Blake's art, Kirkman Gray discovered the same principle at work: imaginative perception correlated to natural phenomena serving the needs of common humanity. Thereupon, he inferred the workings of a cultural idiom in which the aesthetic meant engagement, belonging, and the freedom to collaborate. To this end, he treated Blake's composite art as a meeting place designed to get an audience to imagine new conditions of sociability, a reading of aesthetics pioneered by Ruskin in *The Stones of Venice* (1851–53).[12] Read correctly, *Jerusalem* was not an occultic version of hypotyposis – the idea that the author produces a metadiscursive commentary on his or her ostensible subject, as proposed by Ellis and Yeats in their triadic *The Works of William Blake: Poetic, Symbolic and Critical* (1893) – but a glorious hymn to the open-ended energies of civil liberty and civic kinship:

> For him Art and Citizenship were one … When Blake wandered through the quarters of the city he felt the human significance of what he beheld … To the Blakean imagination every street-cry and every window-blind is alive with the divine comedy of existence. All that gives a thing distinction is human … London is a Man.

> The citizen of London is he who has the inmost quality of London life most clearly fashioned to imaginative power in brain and nerve and blood, whose individual mind thinks with the spiritual meaning of the city.[13]

Blake was thus accorded a privileged insight into the workings of modernity because he brought together perspectives normally kept apart when, trundling through London's chartered streets, he caught a glimpse of spiritual citizenship in the fluxional character of community life.

It is worth pointing out that some aspects of this vision of Blake's heroic combination of personal thought and communal values may have been borrowed from late Victorian and Edwardian accounts of Wordsworthian Romanticism, where the aesthetic is associated with the projection of feeling into the world of public service.[14] Whatever the case, what interests me in Kirkman Gray's unusually inventive and resourceful essay is the movement of an argument in which the city becomes a civilising entity when it is beheld as a living thing, a portal into a world of liberty glimpsed by the dynamic cultural agent.[15] To put this matter into its proper historical context, Kirkman Gray's reading of social history through aesthetics is poles apart from the standard version of urban culture proposed by J. L. and Barbara Hammond, the best-known economic historians of this period. In their influential and popular *Town Labourer* (1917), we find that associational life was eroded by a 'social revolution' produced in the wake of the Industrial Revolution, which reduced the idea of value to what was deemed to be economically productive.[16] In opposition, Kirkman Gray, deploying his civics of vision, imagined that Blake's real subject was the creation of new expressions of liberty. Blake's London, it follows, was both a shared value system and a dynamic energy centre. In effect, Kirkman Gray brought together ethics and vitalism: Blake, the opposite of the charismatic outlaw figure found by Swinburne and Symons, or the mystical subject discovered by Ellis and Yeats, humanised the forces at work in the material world by creating a collective urban pantheism of people, things and habitation, a perfect synthesis of matter and non-matter.

Kirkman Gray's prescient remarks foretold how commentators, in attempting to develop a rationalist model of Blake, could critique the magical reading proposed by Ellis and Yeats; this approach would soon be applied to new critical situations after the posthumous publication of *A Modern Humanist* (1910). The educationalist Joseph Wicksteed exemplifies this strand of humanistic social commentary, where Blake is held to be a civilising agent through his pursuit of liberty. Wicksteed agreed that Ellis and Yeats were peddlers of dangerous pseudo-profundity, but wanted to hold on to their central insight into Blake's art system: his desire for hermeneutic mastery arose from a critical model where perception was interpretative, not representational. The focus of Blake criticism should be, Wicksteed believed, on decoding Blake's mythology through analogical method. Read properly, Blake's art world revealed itself as a set of meaningful details held together by a bodily symbolism of gesture and movement. Wicksteed's *Blake's Vision of the Book of Job* (1910), which was dedicated to the recently deceased Kirkman Gray, is a landmark in Blake studies.[17] All the same, the underlying critical arc of Wicksteed's influential argument has yet to be examined in any real detail. In what follows, I seek to give an account of how Wicksteed contributed to Kirkman Gray's interpretation, which aimed to confound the occultism of the Ellis-Yeats school of criticism by attributing to Blake a consistent method driven by a neo-Christological vision of active citizenship.[18]

While radical theologians like Charles Gardner tended to spotlight the human utopianism of Blake's image of Jesus as the Son of Man, Wicksteed alighted on the story of Job as an expression of human hope.[19] To this end, the humble foot would provide the exegetical ammunition to defeat the critical authority of the esoteric version of Blake. Wicksteed set out to demonstrate that understanding Blake's characterisation of Job was little more than a matter of correlating compositional morphology with a bodily system in which the left foot meant materialism and selfishness, and the right foot meant spiritual vision and liberty. When Blake gave prominence to the left foot this was to confirm a subject corrupted by the belief that the world is a distorted simulacrum of the self; by contrast, when he gave prominence to the right foot, his subject acted as witness to the value of shared human vitality. This symbolism ran throughout Blake's *Illustrations of the Book of Job* (1823–26), Wicksteed proposed.[20] In truth, he set out to demythologise Blake's designs, to reveal that the foot could symbolise free human praxis. Unlike Ellis and Yeats, who saw the Blakean body as an emblematic form driven by his syncretic mentality, Wicksteed believed that the Blakean body was the manifestation of a need to represent citizenship and hospitality.[21] In similar vein, Blake's image world was a place of cooperation and collaboration between producer and viewer. Here, then, was a productively human Blake detached from the need to produce a hermetic system to make good his belief in the critical efficacy of art.[22]

The ramifications of this critical attitude are extremely important; attention moves away from locating meaning in private thinking towards a concern with an external ethical world which regulates and organises the energies of the body. From Wicksteed's point of view, Blake's composite art communicated meaning through modal form; it was not, as articulated by Ellis and Yeats, a set of mystical attributes derived from the wisdom of the perennial philosophy. Notwithstanding occasional exceptions, Blake's art adhered to practical reason and confirmed his collective, developmental model of human subjectivity. For this reason, Wicksteed's version of Blake was immensely attractive to other scholars, since the analogical model defended Blake's symbolism from the hermeneutic machinery imposed on it by the theosophist readings arising from followers of Ellis and Yeats. In place of the mysterious subjectivity of the occult method, Wicksteed reset Blake's pictorial universe as an expression of socio-psychic equilibrium.[23] Seen correctly, Blake's myth-making system oriented itself to public communication by producing an amplified record of human experience. These convictions led Wicksteed to announce that Blake appears 'as one of our great and serious English prophets … It is certain that his work is a treasury of inspired thinking … of quite unsurpassed spiritual insight

… [His] anticipations … of philosophic and ethical ideas that we almost regard as characteristically twentieth century, are scarcely less striking than his alleged poetic anticipations of the great singers of the last century.'[24] Thus understood, Blake at once anticipated and superseded Nietzsche, Tolstoy, Shaw, and other exponents of modern thought.[25] Wicksteed concluded that the dominant theme in Blake's final productions was the reconciliation of the individual life with the universal life of humanity.[26]

What Sydney Style, John Sampson and C. H. Herford contributed to Blake criticism in the first two decades of the twentieth century is an unexplored subject worthy of a separate article. Sydney Style is the most obscure figure in this group. To follow his argument, we must begin by noting that he was a follower of Auguste Comte, and that he presided over the Positivist Church of Humanity in Liverpool between 1908 and 1929. Style's Blake was a rationalist who 'laboured to build Jerusalem'. He understood 'the value of … the in-dwelling Humanity … He recognised the value of science and art … He strove to create from the surrounding chaos of materials a world of beauty and order.'[27] These convictions meant that Blake rejected all forms of professional narrowness in the cultural realm. In accordance with Comtean dicta, Style imagined that the moral force of Blake's synthesising enterprise amounted to a form of trans-historical fellowship: it was pedagogy turned into the science of human cooperation and citizenship, the resetting of historical values in a modern world.[28]

These sociological perceptions were shared by Sampson, chief librarian at the University of Liverpool, who was deeply sympathetic to the production of a rationalised Blake. *The Poetical Works of William Blake* (1905) refers to the 'consistency with which his self-invented system of mythology is expounded and the absolute uniformity with which definite symbolical figures are used to express definite conceptions'. Blake's constructions were 'never arbitrary, but based on system'.[29] By treating the cultural artefact as a self-controlling morphological space, the researcher was in a position to supersede the erroneous readings advanced by Ellis and Yeats, 'whose remarks would seem to suggest their belief that the possession of occult powers enables them to produce a text through which Blake's mind is reflected more accurately than in the MSS, left by himself'. By contrast, Sampson proposed that Blake 'interwove text, design and colouring into one harmonious whole', before concluding that his life was the affirmation of 'mental, moral and artistic harmony'.[30] In describing composite art and aesthetic creativity in these terms, Sampson adhered to positivistic principles, since human achievement is associated with the realisation of the whole of experience. For most Comteans, this condition of universality meant altruism, the marriage of citizenship and hospitality. Blake was in accord with the central node of this scheme since his art of human vitality was a vindication of Comtean philosophy, where the task of humankind was 'the continual improvement of its own nature'.[31]

Some of these matters bubble to the surface of C. H. Herford's long review essay of the Blake centenary exhibition held at the Burlington Fine Art Club (1927).[32] Herford, Professor of English Literature at the University of Manchester, was another important member of the positivist community in the northwest of England.[33] He noted that Blake 'has been something of a local cult' in Liverpool, and then went on to praise Sampson's editing of Blake's writings.[34] Nonetheless, he felt obliged to instruct the reader that Blake struggled to produce coherent pictorial representations of a system where God was a rationalisation of human form, before observing that his art 'obeyed an inner implicit logic of its own, often enough flagrantly at odds with the logic of common sense'. Unsurprisingly, he opined that Blake 'had the inconsistencies … which astute and versatile men avoid, but which are the penalty of elemental natures thrown into a complex and unsympathetic *milieu*. He could be grotesque and sublime, delicately sensitive and outrageously indecent.'[35] Here, as is so often the case in positivistic criticism, the reader is left with the distinct impression that what Herford called Blake's 'imperfectly organized mind' submitted itself to second-order issues it should have ignored.[36] As an afterthought, Herford welcomed the shift from the 'revolutionary anarchism' and 'antinomianism' of *The Marriage of Heaven and Hell* (1790–93) to the Christian humanism of *The Everlasting Gospel* (*c.*1810), which had been reassembled by Sampson. Thereafter, he spelt out the meaning of the work: 'The purport of *The Everlasting Gospel* is not iconoclasm. Blake dismisses the Jesus of evangelicalism in order to vindicate his own "eternal Christ", who could not be humble Himself without also humbling God, and in whom man, participating through imagination, became one with God, and God in him.'[37] At this point, he spotlighted the most 'Comtean' passage in Blake's poem: 'Thou art a man; God is no more/Thy own humanity learn to adore/For that is my own spirit of life.' Blake's significance, therefore, resided in his contribution to broader cultural discourses centring on a humanised Jesus and the concomitant replacement of theology by anthropology.

Ultimately, Herford's assessment, where Blake's contribution to humanistic culture is forever attenuated by the reality of a 'Romantic psychology that repudiated consecutive thinking', should be related to a persistent thread of invective where romantic individualism is identified as the central problem of Blake's aesthetic.[38] By the early decades of the twentieth century this attitude began to acquire new characteristics, as can be seen in the writings of T. S. Eliot.[39] For Eliot, 'Blake was not even a first-rate visionary: his visions have a certain illiteracy about them'. He asks, was Blake 'a great philosopher? No, he did not know enough. He made a Universe; and very few people can do that. But the fact that the gift is rare does not make it necessarily valuable.' At this point, Eliot's judgement is withering: 'it is not any one man's business to make a Universe; and what any one man can make in this way is not, in the end, so good or so useful as the ordinary Universe which we all make together … Isolation is not conducive to correct thinking; and Pride … is, we know, one of the chief theological sins. Blake is philosophically an autodidact amateur; theologically, a heretic.'[40] From Eliot's perspective, Blake's desire to imagine that he has the right to induce readers and viewers to behave in a specific manner confirms that there is nothing hospitable about his art. Dissident individualism, for which Blake gives an exalted justification, is another way of referring to the ontology of solipsism: his inadequate but self-glorifying imagination annihilates nature because it is no more than the reification of an error that begins with the elimination of tradition and custom from any perception of the world and its objects.

Eliot's patrician vision of a coercive and self-sanctifying Blake became something of a critical orthodoxy in the high modernism of the 1920s and 1930s. Richard Aldington, an important member of his literary circle, pre-empted his speculations:

> Those who direct attention to Blake's system and labour to reduce his inchoate ideas to order, do him small service. His system is obviously worthless, the insignificant production of an English dissenter proud, obstinate, uncritical, comparatively uneducated, and ignorant of the elementary principles of philosophy. With the strange arrogance which seems inseparable from this type of mind Blake asserted, and no doubt believed, that truths which are hidden from all mankind had been mysteriously and uniquely revealed to one privileged person, himself ... Yielding to his vanity he presumed to instruct his fellow men concerning the most baffling and hitherto insoluble problems of the universe. And what he had to give was an incoherent mass of mystic guesses and assertions whose fantastic absurdity was hardly lessened by being wrapped up in a mythology of Blake's own invention ... Blake has survived not only his own absurdities, but the efforts of his commentators to rationalize them.[41]

Eliot and Aldington agreed with Alan Porter, who claimed that behind Blake's 'immense cosmography there is no power, no inspiration, no fire ... he was encouraged to take casual errors for everlasting truths, and to centre, not only his own universe, but the universe of universes, in his own monad, his own limited awareness'.[42] For all three writers, then, mythomania explained Blake's inhospitable, quarrelsome character and confirmed why he was unable to produce a naturalistic theory of the world or the mind. In any case, his nebulous thinking could not be trusted because he was not curious enough to acknowledge the reality of the self-deception. The paradigm for what Blake was doing was autotelic expression, the cultural malaise of Romanticism, which reduced the artist to a community of one without external moderators. In sum, the autocratic Blake was akin to a crazed scholar who made weird extrapolations from unverified sources.[43]

The attempts made by Blake's admirers to dispossess Eliot, Aldington, Porter, and other like-minded auditors of their ownership of Blake criticism fall into two categories. In the first category, Blake is little more than a vehicle for inexact and unreliable ethical reflections about the quality of life in the modern world. For Max Plowman, *Songs of Innocence and of Experience* (1794) explains Blake's cultural standing. His Blake, the first citizen in the kingdom of freedom, exults 'self-dependent happiness'. Blake 'discovered childhood. He was the first to announce it. He showed it to be a condition of happiness, unity and self-enjoyment ... he cuts the ground from under our feet ... he freed Western art from slavish adherence to Nature.'[44] This vision, where Blake is a vector for the dissemination of the idea of self-knowledge, was extolled by E. E. Kellet: 'acquaintance with Blake is by itself an enlightenment and an elevation ... For Blake the man was greater than Blake the poet or the painter; and we often feel that to know *him* is enough ... He is sublime with a sublimity of goodness: and those with the germ of goodness in them are awed by him.'[45]

These windy and unstable remarks about heroic self-realisation were of no use to those more exacting Blake admirers who set out to grasp the dynamics of his art system. Darrell Figgis, for example, proposed that the principle of segmental adhesion confirmed that Blake's artistic individualism produced a powerful vision of human generosity and togetherness. Figgis's Blake was a rational subject because consistency was the main feature of his pictorial language. This allowed him to assert that if Blake's designs formed themselves into meaningful aggregations, then they must belong on a cultural spectrum where integration, cooperation and hospitality were the dominant elements. By 1805, Blake 'had … begun to work at his pictures in series, as though no one picture could contain all the thought he desired to convey, a thought that therefore had to utter in a connected series of pictures'. From this he deduced the source of Blake's originality: 'this same overflowing of thought from one design into another, and yet again into another, till it completed itself, and made a unity of the whole, is now found in [situations] even where there is no external unity within which to group a sequence of designs'. Figgis concluded: 'it is as if one picture suggested another on a cognate theme, which he had at once to begin, even when the suggestion was accidental to the designs themselves, not prompted by a coherent thought he wished to convey'.[46] It will be abundantly clear that serialism was not merely a pictorial matter but also a critical one, too, since Figgis insisted that the mature Blake saw his images as unified and continuous forms, equal partners on a spectrum without subsidiary elements; they were affirmations of a formal order driven by the principle of companionship as self-development; and they provided records of visual liberty of immediate value to those individuals concerned with the workings of modern culture.

This critical idiom, which was designed to engage with matters arising from artistic motivation, was developed by Herbert Read, who situated Blake within a larger argument about the trajectory of national cultural history in 'English Art' (1933), published in *The Burlington Magazine*, the premier art journal in the English-speaking world. According to Read, to appreciate the history of English art, it is first necessary to recognise that it adheres to a critical pattern where life forms are opposed to conventional forms. The principle of life is line, expressed through rhythm and fluid pattern. The principle of convention is composition, expressed in the interplay between rational order and visual observation. The art of life originates in Anglo-Saxon material culture, is preserved in the Gothic imagination, and is then annihilated before being magically reborn with Blake; the art of convention arises in the Renaissance from a general receptiveness to the tangible world, becomes incorporated into extra-cultural systems of standardisation and replication, and is then assimilated by the progress-worshipping logic of industrial civilisation. In one respect, Read's argument relates to historical revaluations in F. R. Leavis's *Mass Civilization and Minority Culture* (1930) and, more broadly, R. H. Tawney's *Religion and the Rise of Capitalism* (1926), since all three rejected the conflation of value with industrial enterprise and material prosperity. Another important matter is Read's supposition that Blake's critical sensibility, where art is the translation of imaginative energy into pictorial form, relates to the conflict between vitalist and puritanical elements in the history of English civil and cultural life:

> Blake embodied consciously and consistently the original characteristics of our art … Blake set himself the task of making his vision determinate, of giving imagination an outline. His art is an attempt to combine the greatest intensity of subjective thought and feeling with the greatest clarity of objective representation … Nowhere else in the whole range of plastic art, unless in Giotto, is the capacity of the line for rendering three-dimensional form so amply demonstrated, and nowhere is solidity so compatible with movement and ethereal light. And that is precisely the character of all great art – of classical art in Nietzsche's right conception of it, of Christian art in its Byzantine and early Gothic manifestations, and of the isolated art of an individual like Blake.[47]

Put slightly differently, Blake's 'isolated art' becomes welcoming and universal when it enacts the work of the imagination as realisation of unity of individual experience and collective knowledge.[48] Likewise, the open-endedness of Blake's calligraphic forms invite participation and signal the appearance of a pictorial order based on the principle of free exchange.

This then, roughly, is the model of Blakean liberty proffered by neo-Romantic art criticism. In *British Romantic Artists* (1942), John Piper declares that 'Blake's incantations were rules of life … He was rare simply in his capacity to live fully.'[49] This attitude – where Blake embraces vitality, growth and change – is taken to explain the bucolic exuberance of Samuel Palmer's early works, which, influenced by Blake's Virgil woodcuts, form a magical counterworld to industrial society.[50] In all such discussions, a vision of Blake's independence sits uneasily alongside a model of heteronomy in which meaningful artistic creation is obliged to respond to large problems generated by social modernity. Thomas Hennell and Cecil Collins both agreed that Blake's art was a proto-Ruskinian protest directed at external forces unleashed by industrial society. Hennell's Blake, a particularly complex amalgamation of crafts skills, ruralism and visionary imagination, was situated in a cultural universe opposed to the dominant tradition of productivism in economic life and labour history.[51]

For Collins, too, Blake's 'romantic energy' connects him with a sacred tradition comprising art, work and symbolic vision. To understand Blake is to position him within the history of the culture of hospitality and liberty:

> He was a real voice crying in the wilderness, full of warning of what was coming. He felt already 'the dark satanic mills' of the industrial era. His voice of creative affirmation reaches over a hundred years to take its place in the front line of our modern painters … Society must be based upon our sense of wonder, the one experience which justifies our being alive. Art is a form of transcendental magic which is created out of that awkward sense, and returns to it … It is the direct expression

> of having regained that reverence for all living things which is the only real foundation for human society. When we feel, in the words of that greatest of all surrealist artists, William Blake, 'Everything that Lives is Holy'.[52]

Blake's prophetic tone, if understood correctly, reveals that as all authentic British artists are manifestations of Albion, so all creative vision rejects 'mechanical civilisation'.[53] All along, Blake was a public artist who wanted to be hospitable by contributing to the construction of 'collective mythology', the true purpose of democracy. Yet his desire for a redemptive culture of fellowship was thwarted by the relentlessly menacing powers of the bourgeois section of society. At this point, Collins's fusion of social criticism and political history converges with Bloomfield's address to the Royal Society of Arts:

> The bourgeois persecutes anyone who questions [his view of] reality, either by organised force, like the police, or in England by indifference. This class of people have always existed in one form or another, but since the industrial revolution put a powerful weapon in their hands, they have become stronger and more organised. It is they who have contempt for culture … It is they who have created that vulgar institution the Royal Academy, which represents their idea of culture. It is they who ignored Blake … who burned books of wisdom and poetry … who crucified Christ … and crucified anybody who did not believe in Christ.[54]

In this fantastical picture, Blake, at once primordial power and origin of a way of creating the future through hospitality, functions as the non-assimilable conceptual entity that will defeat the dehumanising forces responsible for the eternal pact between the bourgeoisie and the Nazis.

As this short history of Blake's reception demonstrates, citizenship and hospitality were important elements in the consolidation of his reputation. They remained significant critical categories in post-war commentary when ideas of wholeness, unity and cohesion converged with broader accounts about how defending liberty was the best response to the reality of cultural decline. In fact, it could be argued that all these terms gained urgency as Blake criticism, both mythographic and humanist, expanded through contact with those cultural applications of natural law discourse where the arc of history was seen to bend towards fellowship, justice and the creation of free public knowledge. In these new circumstances, commentators were inclined to propose that the deep purpose of Blake's art was to reveal spiritual kinship with liberal humanism or classical thought, both of which were taken to be under threat in the modern world. In this version of events, a less extroverted Blake stood for the inalienable rights of humankind, and defended human dignity by formulating a viable model of how subjects should think about themselves. According to one well-placed commentator, Blake's visions were 'no escape from reality but an exploration of the spirit, a way of thinking … about the most difficult and complex subjects, the meaning of life, the nature of the human mind and the destiny of mankind'.[55] However much latitude we grant to these bombastic articulations of the post-war 'human condition' discourse, the truth of the matter is that this lexicon of terms created the cultural conditions in which Blake flourished, as evidenced in the collective endeavours of Anthony Blunt, Geoffrey Keynes, Vivian De Sola Pinto, Kathleen Raine, the British Council, the William Blake Trust, and numerous lesser-known cultural commentators, cultural organisations and pressure groups.[56]

Notes

1 See A. Dachev and D. Todman (eds), *War Diaries, 1939–1945: Field Marshall Lord Alanbrooke* (London: Weidenfeld & Nicolson, 2001), p. 105. Alanbrooke was Chief of the Imperial General Staff.

2 Dachev and Todman (eds), *War Diaries, 1939–1945*, pp. 106–8.

3 P. Bloomfield, 'William Blake and his Albion', *Journal of the Royal Society of Arts*, 88 (1940), 845, 846. Bloomfield developed his account of the links between artistic expression and social justice in *The Many and the Few; or, Culture and Destiny* (London: Routledge, 1942).

4 For a capsule summary of concurrent conceptions of Blake's modernity in the United States, see P. Rahv, 'Franz Kafka: The Hero as Lonely Man', *The Kenyon Review*, 1 (1939), 60–74, where Blake's discursivity is contrasted to Kafka's criticality; D. Schwartz, 'Rimbaud in Our Time', *Poetry*, 55 (1939), 148–54, where Blake's epistemology of value predicts Rimbaud's thinking in *A Season in Hell*; and H. R. Hays, 'The Poetry of Bertolt Brecht', *Poetry*, 67 (1945), 148–55, where the social realist aesthetic of *Songs of Experience* anticipates Brecht's reinvention of the ballad form as ironic spikiness. For the bigger picture, see L. Freedman, *William Blake and the Myth of America* (Oxford: Oxford University Press, 2018).

5 This term refers to Blake's illuminated books, such as *The Book of Thel* (1789), *The Marriage of Heaven and Hell* (1790–93), *Visions of the Daughters of Albion* (1793), *The First Book of Urizen* (1794), *Milton* (1804–11) and *Jerusalem* (1820), all of which revived the medieval method of combining image and text in a single page.

6 A. C. Swinburne, *William Blake: A Critical Essay* (London: John Camden Hotten, 1868); A. Symons, *William Blake* (London: A. Constable, 1907). For a detailed discussion of this matter, see C. Trodd, *Visions of Blake: William Blake and the Art World* (Liverpool: Liverpool University Press, 2012), pp. 4–35.

7 A phrase used by R. Ellis Roberts in 'William Blake', *Bookman*, 71 (1927), 274.

8 In his day job, Kirkman Gray was a Unitarian minister and social worker. He joined the Independent Labour Party around 1904.

9 See 'The Mind of a Londoner', in H. B. Binns (ed.), *A Modern Humanist: Miscellaneous Papers by B. Kirkman Gray* (London: A. C. Fifield, 1910), pp. 100–1, 106–7.

10 W. J. T. Mitchell provides a succinct description of *Jerusalem*: 'it is essentially a non-consecutive series of epiphanies or visionary confrontations with the total structure of history … encapsulated in the poet's experience of the personal and historic moments in his own life'. See W. J. T. Mitchell, *Blake's Composite Art* (Princeton, NJ: Princeton University Press, 1978), p. 35.

11 This 'Ruskinian' Blake featured in British political discourse, primarily through the initiatives of a group of thinkers and activists surrounding Clement Atlee, who went on to quote lines from Blake's *Milton* in numerous social and public settings when leader of the opposition and prime minister. See J. Bew, *Clement Atlee: The Man who Made Modern Britain* (Oxford: Oxford University Press, 2017), pp. 116–37, 339–40, 480–1, 507–8.

12 Here, Ruskin argued in favour of what he called 'reciprocal interference', the 'union of one colour with another', 'a magnificent principle', for it was as an instrument of fellowship. See E. T. Cook and A. Wedderburn (eds), *The Works of John Ruskin* (London: George Allen, 1903–12), vol. 11, pp. 23–4.

13 Binns (ed.), *A Modern Humanist*, pp. 110–11, 118–19.

14 For a classic account of the moral integrity of Wordsworthian vision, see L. Stephen, *Hours in a Library* (London: Smith, Elder & Co., 1877), pp. 254–79.

15 Kirkman Gray was assigned the same characteristics in Binns's 'One of London's Lovers', a Whitmanesque prose-poem in honour of his deceased friend. See H. B. Binns, *The Great Companions* (New York: B. H. Huebsch, 1911), pp. 45–50. Binns was the author of *A Life of Walt Whitman* (1905), the first biographical work to appear after the poet's death in 1892.

16 J. L. and B. Hammond, *Town Labourer* (London: Longmans, Green & Co., 1917).

17 J. Wicksteed, *Blake's Vision of The Book of Job* (London: J. M. Dent & Sons Limited, 1910).

18 Wicksteed had expressed similar ideas at the London Society for the Study of Religion, which he established in 1904.

19 C. Gardner, *Vision & Vesture* (London: J. M. Dent & Sons Limited, 1916); and *William Blake: The Man* (London: J. M. Dent & Sons Limited, 1919).

20 Wicksteed, *Blake's Vision*, pp. 133–6.

21 Wicksteed went on to become headmaster at St Alfred's School, Hampstead, between 1921 and 1933.

22 This part of his argument may have been designed to counter Laurence Binyon's well-known claim that Blake lacked 'sympathetic humanism'. See L. Binyon (ed.), *William Blake: Illustrations of the Book of Job* (London: Methuen and Co., 1906), p. xii.

23 This definition of the Blakean body as system of codified gestures was developed in the post-war period by George Wingfield Digby, Geoffrey Keynes, Albert S. Roe and Janet Warner.

24 Wicksteed, *Blake's Vision*, p. 14.

25 *Ibid.*, p. 14. For an account of the history of the 'Nietzschean' Blake, see C. Trodd, 'The Energy Man: Blake, Nietzscheanism and Cultural Criticism in Britain, 1890–1920', *Visual Culture in Britain*, 19 (2018), 298–304.

26 Wicksteed, *Blake's Vision*, pp. 24–5. See also Gardner, *William Blake: The Man*; and J. Middleton Murry, *William Blake* (London: Jonathan Cape, 1936), both of whom present Blake as an antidote to the ego-theism of modern society.

27 See S. Style, *Paradise Lost by John Milton with Illustrations by William Blake* (Liverpool: Liverpool Booksellers, 1906), p. vii. Style, a wealthy solicitor, owned an impressive collection of Blake paintings.

28 See O. Baier, *In Memoriam: Sydney Style* (privately printed, 1930), p. 10, where Style is remembered as 'a student of Blake's creative genius' who understood how Blake's art relates to Comte's writings.

29 J. Sampson (ed.), *The Poetical Works of William Blake* [1904] (London: Oxford University Press, 1913), pp. x, viii. This edition of Blake's writings was praised as 'a masterpiece of editing' in *The Athenaeum*, 4083 (1906), 100.

30 *Ibid.*, pp. xxviii, xv, xix.

31 See T. R. Wright, *The Religion of Humanity: The Impact of Comtean Positivism on Victorian London* (Cambridge: Cambridge University Press, 1986), p. 22.

32 C. H. Herford, 'William Blake', *Bulletin of the John Rylands Library*, 12 (1928), 31–46. See also R. Hinks, 'Art Chronicle: The Century of William Blake', *The Criterion*, 6 (1927), 431–6. The Blake exhibition at the Burlington Fine Art Club is reviewed by Trodd, *Visions of Blake*, pp. 448–51.

33 See Herford, 'Appreciation', in Baier, *In Memoriam*, pp. 18–20.

34 Herford, 'William Blake', p. 32.

35 *Ibid.*, p. 32.

36 *Ibid.*, p. 34.

37 *Ibid.*, p. 44. This perception relates to Sampson's account of *Jerusalem*, which he reads as a 'daring and beautiful perversion of the *Agnus Dei*'. See Sampson, *The Poetical Works*, p. 372.

38 For an account of this literature, see Trodd, *Visions of Blake*, pp. 13–229.

39 T. S. Eliot, 'Blake', *The Sacred Wood* (London: Methuen and Co. Limited, 1920), pp. 128–34; 'The Mysticism of Blake', *The Nation & Athenaeum*, 41 (1927), 779.

40 Eliot, 'The Mysticism of Blake', 779. This notice – a review of publications by Geoffrey Keynes, Mona Wilson, Max Plowman and Helen C. White – develops a point made in his letter to Richard Aldington (March 1927), where Blake is dismissed as 'a chapter in the History of Hersey (my great underwritten work in 15 vols. qto)'. See, V. Eliot and J. Haffenden (eds), *The Letters of T. S. Eliot, Volume 3: 1926–7* (London: Faber & Faber, 2012), p. 436.

41 R. Aldington, 'William Blake', *The Nation & Athenaeum*, 40 (1927), 858. Virginia Woolf's husband was equally immune to the appeal of Blake's work: 'in the prophetic books he is … the expounder and explainer and priest of some esoteric mystical doctrine and dogma which has to be deliberately shrouded in veils of symbolism and obscurity … I cannot become his pupil or one of his congregation, for I see no reason to believe that … William Blake can give me eternal truth in some patent pill.' See L. Woolf, 'William Blake', *The Nation & Athenaeum*, 37 (1925), 649.

42 A. Porter, 'The Company of Dragons', *The Spectator*, 132 (1924), 922. He developed this criticism in 'Prophecy Without Pains', *The Spectator*, 136 (1926), 1086: 'His doctrine cannot even be called Anarchic, for Anarchism is at least a theory of the associations and conflicts of human beings; it has a place in sociology. Blake was much more radically an individualist; he never even considered the fact that other wills were as much entitled to freedom as his own.'

43 See R. Fry, *Reflections on British Painting* (London: Faber & Faber, 1934), pp. 173–6.

44 M. Plowman, *An Introduction to the Study of William Blake* (London: J. M. Dent & Sons, 1927), pp. 68–9, 11–12, 19–20.

45 E. E. Kellett, 'The Pilgrim of Eternity', *New Statesman*, 29 (1927), 572. See also E. Underhill, 'The Spectre and the Emanation', *Spectator Literary Supplement*, 141 (1928), 532: 'whatever be the *meaning* of Blake's designs, one feels they are themselves greater than their meaning. They offer us news from a realm that lies beyond thought'.

46 D. Figgis, *The Paintings of William Blake* (London: Ernest Benn Ltd, 1925), p. 65.

47 H. Read, 'English Art', *Burlington Magazine*, 63 (1933), 260, 269.

48 The modelling of Blake as magus of pan-spirituality is beyond the scope of this article. Nonetheless, see A. Coomaraswamy, *Dance of Shiva* (New Delhi and London: Asia Publishing House, 1918), pp. 22–3, 32–3, 155–6; L. Binyon, 'The Western Spirit in Art', *Saturday Review of Politics, Literature, Science and Art*, 109 (1910), 753; and J. Gould Fletcher, 'Blake's Affinities with Oriental Thought', *The Aryan Path* (1930), 581–6, and especially 582–3, where he notes the 'striking affinity of Los with Shiva, who is alternately destroyer and regenerator … [Blake's work] proves that the possibility exists that Eastern and Western views of Life may be brought into contact'.

49 J. Piper, *British Romantic Artists* (London: Collins, 1942), p. 28.

50 *Ibid.*, pp. 29–31.

51 Hennell's idiosyncratic painting of the Battle of Britain (private collection, *c.*1941) amplifies Bloomfield's vision by imagining a folkic pastoral, derived from Blake's *Nurse's Song*, where the aerial invasion of the south of England is repelled by children dancing around a maypole.

52 C. Collins, 'The Artist in Society', lecture, 1941, in Brian Keeble (ed.), *Cecil Collins: The Vision of the Fool and other Writing* (London: Golgonooza Press, 2002), pp. 68, 86.

53 *Ibid.*, p. 69.

54 *Ibid.*, p. 71.

55 V. De Sola Pinto, 'William Blake: The Visionary Man', *Journal of the Royal Society of Arts*, 106 (1958), 80.

56 G. Keynes, *Blake* (London: Faber & Faber, 1945), *Blake: Complete Writings with Variant Reading* (Oxford: Oxford University Press, 1966); K. Raine, *Blake* (London: British Council, 1951), *Blake and Tradition*, 2 vols (Princeton: Princeton University Press, 1968), *Blake* (London: Thames & Hudson, 1970); V. De Sola Pinto (ed.), *The Divine Image: Studies in the Poetry & Art of William Blake by Scholars from Three Continents* (London: Victor Gollancz Ltd, 1957); A. Blunt, *The Art of William Blake* (New York: Columbia University Press, 1959); G. Goyder, 'The Origins of the William Blake Trust', *Blake/An Illustrated Quarterly*, 21 (1988), 150–1; and C. Trodd, 'Celebration and Censure: William Blake and Stories of Masterliness in the British Art World, 1930–59', in S. Clark, T. Connolly and J. Whittaker (eds), *Blake 2.0* (Basingstoke: Palgrave Macmillan, 2012), pp. 91–101.

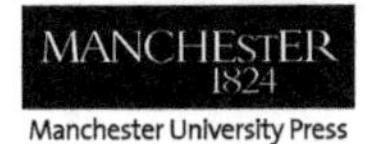

Manchester University Press

Avant-Garde Blake: From Francis Bacon To *Oz* Magazine

DAVID HOPKINS, UNIVERSITY OF GLASGOW

Abstract
This article discusses how we might formulate an account of William Blake's avant-garde reception. Having dealt with Peter Bürger's theorisation of the notion of 'avant-garde', it concentrates on a series of portraits, made from Blake's life mask, by Francis Bacon in 1955. This 'high art' response to the Romantic poet is then contrasted with a series of 'subcultural' responses made from within the British counterculture of the 1960s. Case studies are presented from the alternative magazine production of the period (notably an illustration from *Oz* magazine in which Blake's imagery is conflated with that of Max Ernst). An article by David Widgery in *Oz* on Adrian Mitchell's play *Tyger* (1971) is also discussed to show how the scholarly literature on Blake of the period (mainly David Erdman) was called on by the counterculture to comment on political issues (e.g. Enoch Powell's 1968 'Rivers of Blood' speech). The final section of the article shows how the 'avant-gardism' of *Oz*'s utilisation of Blake might be counterposed to the more activist left-wing approach to the poet in small magazines such as *King Mob* with their links to French situationism. In terms of the classic avant-garde call for a reintegration of art and life-praxis, such gestures testify to a moment in the 1960s when Blake may be considered fully 'avant-garde'.

Keywords: William Blake; reception; Francis Bacon; surrealism; avant-garde; subculture; *Oz* magazine; *King Mob* magazine

This article concerns the way the artistic reception of William Blake changed in Britain between the 1950s and the early 1970s; but initially, a few introductory points need to be made. In the 1930s, Blake's impact might be seen as straddling the neo-Romantic revival of pastoralism (which took Blake's 'disciple' Samuel Palmer as its main figurehead) and British surrealism's emphasis on the visionary aspects of Blake's work.[1] In the current context, it is the surrealist reading of Blake that initially concerns us, since it provides an opening on to the later 'avant-garde' conception of the poet and artist. There has been little analytical work on Blake in these terms until now. His importance for modernists and postmodernists, such as the American Beat poets of the 1950s and 1960s or the *Children of Albion* poets assembled in Britain by Michael Horovitz at the end of the 1960s (an issue that will be touched on again later in this article) has been frequently acknowledged, but little attention has been given to how Blake's reception in such 'avant-garde' terms came about.[2] Given that surrealism has been pinpointed by theorists as a paradigmatic instance of avant-gardism, it makes sense to start with a few thoughts about Blake's surrealist reception – primarily in relation to the movement's French manifestation, but also in its rather diluted form in Britain.[3] This will set the scene for Blake's late-twentieth-century British avant-garde reception.

Bulletin of the John Rylands Library, Volume 98, No. 1 (Spring 2022), pp. 55–73, published by Manchester University Press.
http://dx.doi.org/10.7227/BJRL.98.1.6

It is necessary to begin with a working definition of what 'avant-garde' means. The term tends to be bandied around rather loosely, and is often made to appear synonymous with the technical and stylistic experimentalism characteristic of much early twentieth-century modernist cultural practice. However, in the most rigorous exploration of the concept – in Peter Bürger's book *Theory of the Avant-Garde* (1984) – 'avant-garde' is made to stand for something that goes far beyond the development of new artistic languages (although a dissatisfaction with past forms and a commitment to experimentalism are often among its identifying features). Drawing heavily on Marxist theory, especially Adorno, Bürger argues that what truly characterised what he calls the 'historical avant-garde' was an attack on the 'institution of art' in so far as that was bound up with a notion of aesthetic autonomy:

> The concept of 'art as an institution' as used here refers to the productive and distributive apparatus and also to the ideas about art that prevail at a given time and that determine the reception of works. The avant-garde turns against both – the distributive apparatus on which the work of art depends, and the status of art in bourgeois society as defined by the concept of autonomy. Only after art, in nineteenth century Aestheticism, has altogether detached itself from the praxis of life can the aesthetic develp 'purely'. But the other side of autonomy, art's lack of social impact, also becomes recognizable. The avant-gardiste protest, whose aim is to reintegrate art into the praxis of life, reveals the nexus between autonomy and the absence of any consequences.[4]

In Bürger's terms, then, art's aesthetic detachment from what, in this brief quotation, he loosely describes as 'consequences' (i.e. social effects) can only be countered by a process of reintegration. Elsewhere he describes this as the 'the sublation of art' into the praxis of life. According to this concept, 'art was not simply to be destroyed, but transferred to the praxis of life where it would be preserved, albeit in changed form', but Bürger warns that the concern of the avant-garde was not merely to fit art to an existing praxis: 'On the contrary, they [the avant-gardists] assent to the aestheticist's rejection of the world and its means–end rationality. What distinguishes them from the latter is the attempt to organize a new life praxis on the basis of art.'[5]

Bürger's theory was largely developed to characterise the concerns of early twentieth-century art movements for which the continuation of 'art-for-art's sake' attitudes (or 'Aestheticism' in Bürger's terms) was an anathema: Dada, surrealism, futurism and constructivism. For such movements, art in the modern age could only be understood as effective if it attempted a radical structural intervention in the social and political spheres. It therefore resisted art's consignment, under market capitalism, to the spheres of bourgeois taste and consumption. In the case of the left-leaning movements, such as surrealism and constructivism, this meant that art's destiny was ultimately aligned with communist ideology, in the service, supposedly, of 'transforming life'.[6]

The demand that art should engage itself so closely with lived experience that it effectively dissolved itself and reconfigured itself as praxis (hence producing the 'sublation' of Bürger's definition) was a particularly stringent one – and surrealism, in so far as it failed to convincingly align itself with the communist cause in the 1930s, arguably found itself unequal to the task.[7] Among artists of the later twentieth century, who were disparaged by Bürger as the 'neo-avant-garde', the imperative of avant-gardism was often reduced to the rather nebulous idea of a merger of art and life.[8] But, even when the avant-garde failed to align itself meaningfully with politics – and that was frequently the case in the practices of individual Dadaists and surrealists – to be 'avant-garde' required that, in some significant sense, the artist face up to the material conditions determing the nature of modern life, whether mass culture, technological change or new forms of consciousness were at stake.

To return to British surrealism it might easily be asserted that it fell far short of Bürger's definition. The British group did not, for instance, show much interest in communist thought and in many ways British surrealism's theoretical elaboration, in works such as Herbert Read's book *Surrealism* (1936), simply show it rehashing Romanticism. In respect of the latter, it was largely in Romantic terms that Blake was taken up by artists, particularly by the likes of Paul Nash.[9] However, it might equally be argued that one figure associated with the British movement did at least begin to nudge Blake into a confrontation with the material conditions of modern life. Although research on Humphrey Jennings, both as a surrealist and a Blakean, is still in its infancy, it seems that he was unique in aligning the machinist iconography of Dada and surrealism with Blake's earlier ambivalent response to the energies of the Industrial Revolution (a reading of Blake that partly derived from Jennings's familiarity with Jacob Bronowski's writings on the artist).[10]

This fundamentally materialist reception of Blake within British modernism has been accorded scant attention, but it paved the way for the most compelling response to Blake in post-war British art: Eduardo Paolozzi's huge sculpture, *Newton* (1995) which now stands outside the British Library in London. Paolozzi inherited from Jennings the sense of Blake, not so much as a seer or visionary, but as someone who grappled with the psychical and material shifts brought about via the introduction of the machine in the industrial age. In Paolozzi's re-interpretation of Blake's famous *Newton* print of 1795 we are presented with an image of the body-as-machine, which compellingly updates the Romantic poet's remarkable images of the energised body in late-twentieth century terms. What is more, in this image (to borrow Blakean phraseology) Paolozzi's Newton takes on the lineaments of avant-gardism: the spiritualised Blakean body is literally 'metallised', encased in what looks like armour and brought into a provocative conjunction with technology.

Paolozzi's machinist/materialist response to Blake is a fairly isolated instance. Surprisingly, Paolozzi rarely alluded to Blake in any other aspects of his work, and there is little else in the reception of Blake in the British painting and sculpture of the 1950s and 1960s that qualifies as a bona fide avant-garde response to the Romantic poet. However, one peculiar instance of Blake's take-up in this period should be considered in some detail, as it features in the work of an artist many would certainly consider to be 'avant-garde', the British painter Francis Bacon (although, as we shall see, the label may be mis-applied in this case). On the face of it, Bacon, the creator

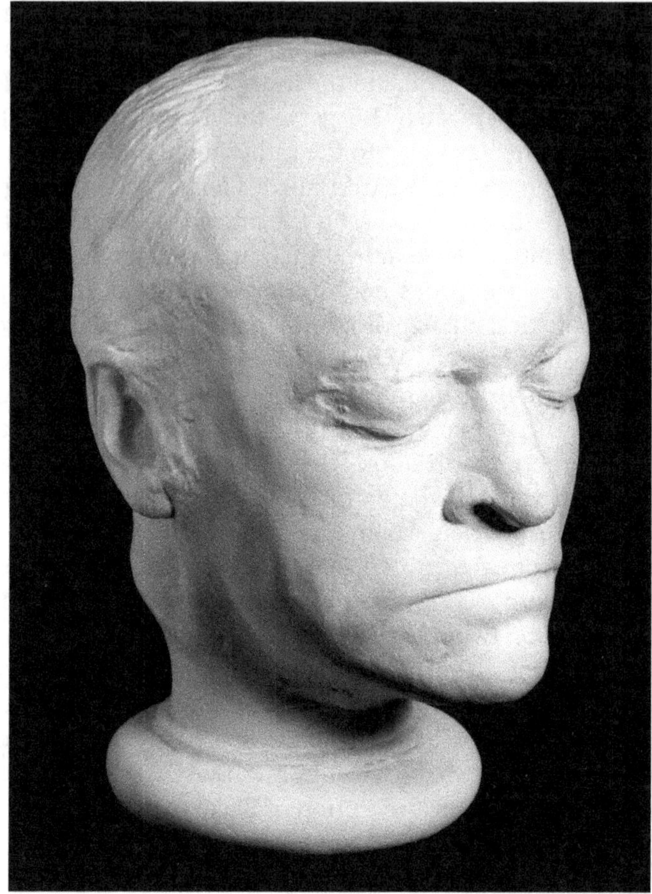

Figure 1 *Head of William Blake*, plaster cast by James Deville, 1823. Courtesy of National Portrait Gallery, London.

of fiercely distorted and animalistic images of the human form (the ubiquitously reproduced *Three Studies for Figures at the Base of a Crucifixion* of 1946 being one example) would seem the least likely figure to have inherited anything from Blake; the temperaments of the two artists were so far apart. Yet, in 1955 Bacon produced a series of six paintings, based on a life mask of Blake, that constitutes one of the most intriguing responses to the Romantic poet and artist of the post-war era.

The story behind the production of Blake's life mask is, in the first place, fascinating. It was originally made in 1823 from the then 66-year-old artist and poet by James Deville, a sculptor and phrenologist employed by the sought-after Neoclassical sculptor Joseph Nollekens. Although the exact reason for the cast's production is hard to determine, it may well have assisted in phrenological researches; the shape of Blake's head epitomising for Deville the 'imaginative faculties'.[11] Whatever the case, it was an ordeal for Blake; in order to make the cast he had to breathe through two straws inserted into his nose. The plaster reportedly pulled out a quantity of his hair: hence the unnatural downward curve of the mouth, supplying him with a stern expression that was completely at odds with his normal disposition.[12]

Francis Bacon encountered the head in 1955 in the National Portrait Gallery in London. At the time he was wrestling with a commission to produce a cover illustration for a score by a friend of his, the composer Gerard Schurmann, titled 'Nine Poems of William Blake' (later to be reworked, in 1996–97, as 'Six Songs of William Blake'). Schurmann apparently took Bacon to see the bust, but, in the end, in line with Bacon's habitual preference for working from reproductions, the six paintings were based on black and white photographs obtained from the gallery. Schurmann's score was not eventually published, but Bacon was happy enough with the paintings to exhibit them at the Hanover Gallery, London, in 1957.[13]

Bacon's attitude to Blake is not easy to determine. He once acknowledged his respect for Blake as a poet, but seems to have been little drawn to his visual art and generally felt little sympathy for what he termed the poet/artist's 'mystical side'.[14] Broadly speaking, he may simply have seen Blake, a Londoner like himself, as a cultural precursor to be measured up to – in the course of his career, Bacon pursued artistic dialogues with figures as diverse as Velázquez, Van Gogh and T. S. Eliot.

Concentrating on the painting from the sequence which critics have tended to see as the most resolved and which is now part of the Tate collection, *Study for Portrait II: after the Life Mask of Willam Blake* (1955), Bacon responded most readily to Blake's severe expression and the grim set of the mouth. This may well have chimed with Bacon's own residual pessimism. Beyond this, the quality of the paint-handling deserves special attention. Characteristically, Bacon appears to have smeared and dragged the paint – using rags or bits of card as much as brushes – around the form of the face and neck. Jonathan Jones describes the resultant image as a 'pale film in the dark, a flayed face, features compressed like those of a bank robber with a stocking over his head', adding that 'it's as if we are looking underneath the surface of skin at the ghostly presence of the man within'.[15]

This sense that the image is one of the 'inner man' is underlined by the realisation that, in the mid-1950s, Bacon's filmy passages of paint owed something to the strange photographic imagery relating to spiritualist practices he encountered in a book that particularly obsessed him: Baron von Schrenck-Notzing's *Phenomena of Materialisation* (1920). Here, as one writer explains, 'white blobs of ectoplasm, the supposed viscous substance exuded by the spiritualist medium during a trance, emerge from the mediums and float freely across the air'.[16] Such imagery was clearly translated by Bacon into the tissue-like skeins of paint found in such other mid-1950s paintings as *The End of the Line* (1953).[17] In the Blake head, it is quite possible that the flayed, bluish-white, X-ray-like appearance of the face also bears some relation to ectoplasmic imagery. This is reinforced by the likelihood that Bacon would have known that Blake's reputation as a 'visionary' had spiritualist connotations. Blake was known to have been visited by spirits and to have drawn portraits from them such as *The Man Who taught Blake Painting in his Dreams* (*c.*1819–20) or, more notoriously, *The Ghost of a Flea* (1819–20). What is even more intriguing

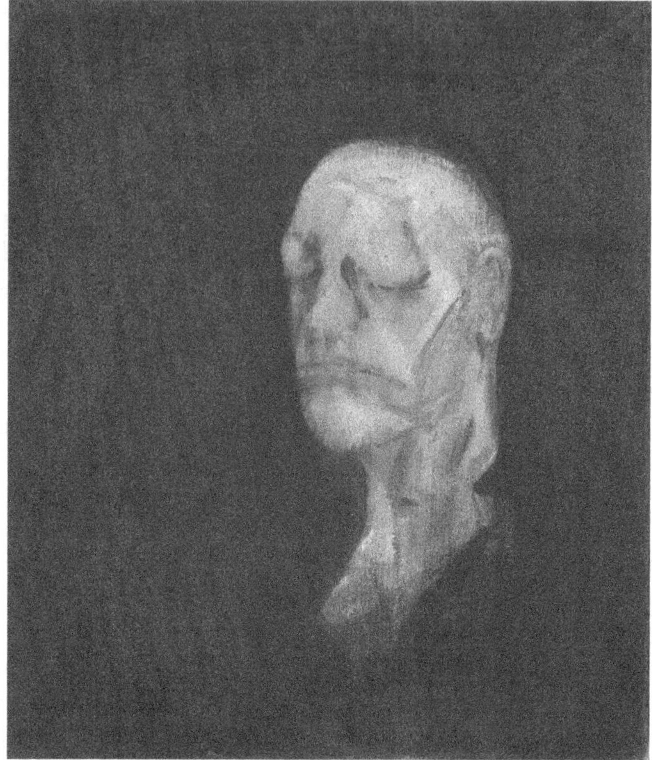

Figure 2 Francis Bacon, *Study for Portrait II (After the Life Mask of William Blake)*, oil on canvas, 1955.

is that such spiritualism-related images by Blake had already made their mark on avant-garde practice. Certain of Joan Miró's painted and drawn self-portraits of the 1920s and 1930s borrowed very directly from the hieratic gaze of *The Man Who Taught Blake Painting*, for example.[18] All of this suggests that, much as Bacon may have produced a sadistic, uncompromising image of a bleakly pessimistic Blake in his 1955 studies, he was actually drawing on a fairly conventional 'surrealist' understanding of the visionary poet/artist. If anything the gesture leans towards the Romantic interiority of the surrealist legacy than the more socially responsive 'avant-garde' side represented by the machinist/surrealist practices of Jennings and Paolozzi.

As already noted, Bacon's remarkable homage, like Paolozzi's *Newton*, was very much a one-off gesture. Possibly, like Paolozzi's later sculpture, it suggests the limits of what could be done in response to the great Romantic in the increasingly rarefied languages of late modernist painting/sculpture in the 1950s–1970s. To move forward in this discussion, it seems necessary to step outside the high-cultural confines of Fine Art, and to appreciate that the construction of an avant-garde Blake occurred more decisively in the expanded popular culture of the period. To understand how

Blake could remain relevant as a cultural force in later twentieth-century Britain requires a methodological shift from the study of high art to mass culture; this being in line with shifts in the nature of 'culture' itself in the period, from something belonging to an elite to something consumed by a more class-variegated audience – as defined by commentators on post-war British society such as Raymond Williams, Richard Hoggart and Stuart Hall.[19]

The theoretical moves involved in showing how the high culture of mid-twentieth-century Britain underwent transformation at the hands of what Theodor Adorno and Max Horkheimer once derisively termed the 'culture industry' – involving the diffusion of elite tastes and values into the wider culture via the technological expansion of capitalism and the shifts in class configurations bound up with that process – would be far outside the scope of this article.[20] One aspect of that overall shift was the creation of what Stuart Hall and the cultural studies theorists in Birmingham in the 1970s termed 'subcultures'. Without entering into the detail of their arguments, they used concepts such as the 'embourgeoisement' of working-class youth and the structural displacement of a dominant 'parent' culture by a disaffected younger generation to develop a model of the way 'youth' became a decisive factor in the reception and reorganisation of values in culture-at-large from the 1950s onwards. According to Hall and his co-authors:

> In modern societies, the most fundamental groups are the social classes, and the cultural configurations will be, in a fundamental though often mediated way, 'class cultures'. Relative to these cultural-class configurations, *sub*-cultures are subsets – smaller [...] more differentiated structures, within one or other of the larger cultural networks of which they form a distinctive part. When we examine the relationship between a 'subculture' and the 'culture' of which it is part, we call the latter the 'parent' culture. This must not be confused with a particular relationship between 'youth' and their 'parents' [...]. What we mean is that a subculture, though differing in important ways – in its 'focal concerns', its peculiar shapes and activities – from the culture from which it derives, will also share something in common with that 'parent' culture.[21]

Interestingly, they then go on to align the concept of subculture with the notion of the avant-garde:

> The bohemian subculture of the *avant-garde* which has arisen from time to time in the modern city, is both distinct from its 'parent' culture (the urban culture of the middle class intelligentsia) and yet also part of it (sharing with it a modernising outlook, standards of education, a privileged position vis-à-vis productive labour, and so on).[22]

Following on from this, one would be justified in expecting avant-gardism to have migrated into subcultural forms in the context of the 1950s and 1960s, and it is not surprising that the avant-garde/surrealist reception of Blake arguably underwent its most productive flowering not in the rarefied sphere of late-modernist art, but in the 'low cultural' sphere of countercultural magazine production. The contention in the second half of this article will thus be that it is in the context of the so-called 'counterculture' of the 1960s – understood to be a form of 'subculture', although its largely middle-class membership meant that it was closer to the cultural elite than the predominantly working-class subcultures studied by Hall *et al.* – that we can best appreciate how Blake could become part of the late twentieth-century 'sublation' of art into the 'praxis of life'.[23]

Britain's counterculture epoch is usually dated from 1965, with the Albert Hall poetry reading of June that year in which the Blake-inspired American poet Allen Ginsberg was a prominent performer, acting as the symbolic focus for a small group of 'underground' British poets including Jeff Nuttall, Alexander Trocchi and Michael Horovitz. To begin with, this subcultural shift was one of mental attitudes rather than politics. In Britain, political dissent in the 1950s had largely centred around the Campaign for Nuclear Disarmament (CND), but disillusionment with the British Left in the early 1960s led to a situation in which, according to Peter Stansill and David Zane Mairowitz, recalling the period in 1971:

> The gloomy earnestness of the 'protest' mentality [was] displaced by a new 'tough' frivolity and creative lunacy [...] the debate [was] no longer between Right Wing/Left Wing, but rather between the oppressions of the external world and the desire for internal liberation.[24]

By 1968, the 'psychedelic' phase of this movement was underway. Experimentation with drugs, and a radical music culture went hand in hand with the assimilation of various currents of early twentieth-century avant-garde thought: pre-eminently Dada, surrealism and French situationism. As is regularly noted, anything from Art Nouveau to the surrealism of Dalí and Ernst stood to be plundered by the counter-culture's art directors and designers. At the same time, psychologists and political theorists such as R. D. Laing, Wilhelm Reich and Herbert Marcuse acquired an unprecedented popular currency as critics of the repressive effects of familial and social structures and as advocates of libidinal rights.

In the wake of the May 1968 events in Paris, the character of the counterculture in Britain shifted markedly. The art historian Andrew Wilson notes that events such as the occupation of the London School of Economics in 1967, along with opposition to America's involvement in the Vietnam War, brought the 'counterculture' alongside the politics of the New Left. The exploration of inner space was gradually abandoned in favour of an idiosyncratic mix of political and esoteric concerns on the part of the 'alternative society'. Wilson supplies a useful list of the causes that were now at stake:

> Black power and the campaign for racial equality; the personal explorations prescribed by drug culture as well as the struggle for sexual liberation with the rise of feminism and the gay liberation movement; the fight against censorship and obscenity laws [...] other liberation movements for which Che Guevara had become an icon and which became polarized around protests against the different struggles in Vietnam, South Africa and Northern Ireland; alternative living, from communes

to the squatting movements, from ecology to new age mysticism, vegetarianism, ley lines and the quest for Atlantis.[25]

All of this covers only a few years of intense countercultural activity, from about 1966 to 1972. My concern from this point on is to look at how Blake's reception became entangled in this. The emphasis will be on underground magazines, the main organs for the popular dissemination of countercultural thought, with close attention paid to the notorious *Oz* magazine, published between 1967 and 1973. Although there is no space to discuss the ramifications of this from a methodological angle, it will become clear that rather than using the art historical or literature studies approach one might normally expect from Blake criticism, it is more appropriate to use what, in the last couple of decades, has been variously termed a 'material studies' or 'visual culture' methodology, focusing on the way 'low cultural' artefacts are consumed as part of social processes. Whereas the discussion of Blake's reception by Paolozzi or Bacon could easily fall under the remit of 'art history' as it is traditionally conceived, to talk of Blake's take-up in countercultural publications necessitates an approach more akin to 'visual culture' studies.[26] Magazines, by their very nature, are inexpensive, mass-circulation products without pretensions to refined aesthetic appeal. As such they are ideal vehicles for the re-circulation and recontextualising of high-cultural imagery for subcultural consumption.

To return, then, to *Oz*. Now notorious as the magazine whose flagrant use of supposedly obscene imagery in the so-called 'School Kids' issue of April 1970 resulted in one of the longest-lasting obscenity trials in British history, it is a very good indicator of the countercultural politics of its period. Having started in its British form under the editorship of the Australian Richard Neville, it rapidly moved from being a kind of *Private Eye*-style satirical magazine to a venue for eye-catching psychedelic graphics, courtesy of its designer, the Australian Pop artist Martin Sharp. In this respect it stood out from its sister magazine, *International Times*, arguably a slightly more sober countercultural vehicle, which had been born before *Oz* in 1966.

Martin Sharp's interventions in an early issue of the magazine, no. 23 of August/September 1969, give a good indication of the character of the publication. Initially, the cover gives us some clue as to what to expect inside. It shows two men – one white, one black – embracing, with a quotation from Oscar Wilde's 'Ballad of Reading Gaol' placed beneath the image: 'yet each man kills the thing he loves' (possibly an allusion to the assassination of Martin Luther King and subsequent race riots in America in the previous year, but probably intended as a more general swipe at racist ideology). The 'O' of the magazine's title, at the top left, has been replaced with an image of the moon and below that, at the bottom left of the main illustration, is a small graphic illustration of an eagle.

Inside the magazine, the various clues on the cover are cashed in. A few pages into the issue there is another photograph of the two men from the cover locked in an embrace; this time it is captioned 'Man Maketh Man.'[27] This was a clear provocation that went beyond the racial intermixing figured in the image to the question

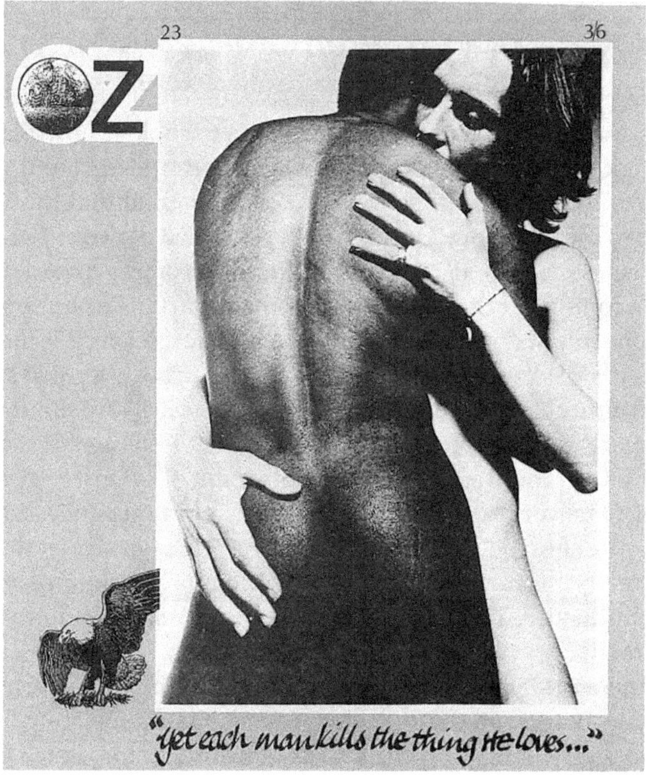

Figure 3 Cover of *Oz* magazine, no. 23, August/September 1969. Private collection.

of gay rights. The Sexual Offences Act of two years earlier had overturned the illegality of homosexuality in Britain (although related sexual acts were still forbidden to those under 21 years of age), but there remained widespread anti-gay discrimination. In the same year as this issue of *Oz*, the 'Campaign for Homosexual Equality' was launched. A few pages later there is an article by Robert Hughes, then an occasional contributor to the magazine, like his Australian counterpart Germaine Greer. Hughes concentrates on another issue of political significance, this time a very recent event: the American moon landing that had occurred on 20 July 1969. In combative style, he sees the event as an act of cosmic colonialism on the part of the USA, noting that the planting of the US flag on the moon was significantly at odds with the idea that the moon, according to an international agreement of 1967, was international territory.[28]

How then does Blake enter into this lively discursive matrix? As we will see, it is only obliquely: by the back door, so to speak. Spread over a few pages inside the magazine is a suite of flagrant appropriations by Martin Sharp from a German edition of the surrealist Max Ernst's collage novel *La Femme 100 Têtes* of 1927, captioned with Sharp's hand-written translations from the German version of Ernst's

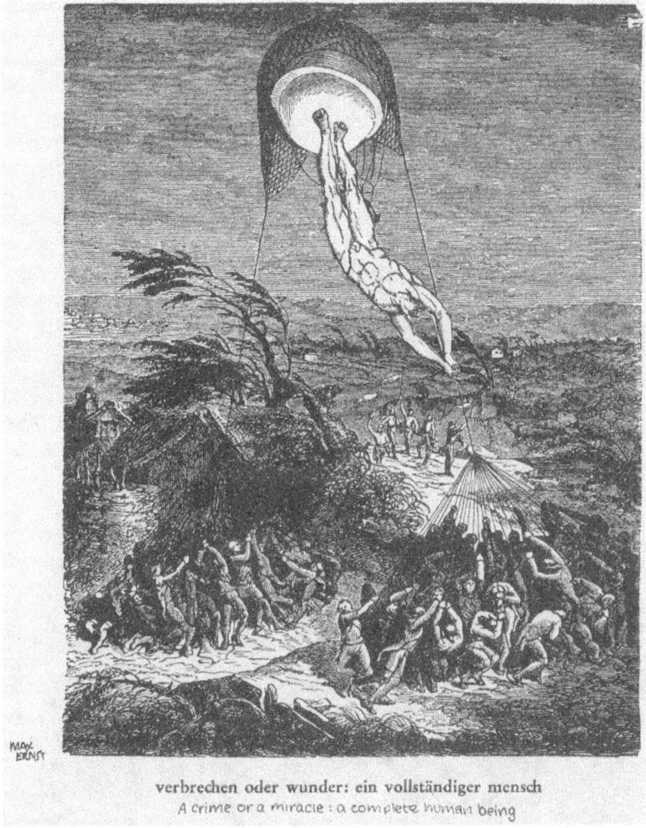

Figure 4 Appropriation of Max Ernst: 'Crime or Miracle: a complete human being' (from *La Femme 100 Têtes*, 1929) by Martin Sharp, *Oz* magazine, no. 23, August/September 1969, p. 5. Private collection.

publication.[29] In one of these, Sharp appropriates from Ernst's own previous appropriations.[30] Ernst himself had borrowed two images to make up his original collage: first, that of a group of men who appear to have netted some enormous airborne object and are hauling it down to the ground (possibly an illustration from a Jules Verne novel), and second, a reversed image from Blake's title page to Robert Blair's *The Grave* of 1808, showing a naked man (symbolic of the human soul) descending from the heavens. What Sharp did, of course, in re-using Ernst's image, was bring together the two thematic strands from this issue of the magazine that have just been discussed: the moon landing (which is hinted at by the extra-terrestrial body in the sky) and homosexuality (signified by the nude male from Blake, whose presence is surely commented on in the appropriated title from Ernst's original collage: 'Crime or Miracle: a complete human being').

Blake, then, was being drafted into the magazine – courtesy of one of the most esteemed avant-garde figures of the 1920s and 1930s, Max Ernst – to comment on

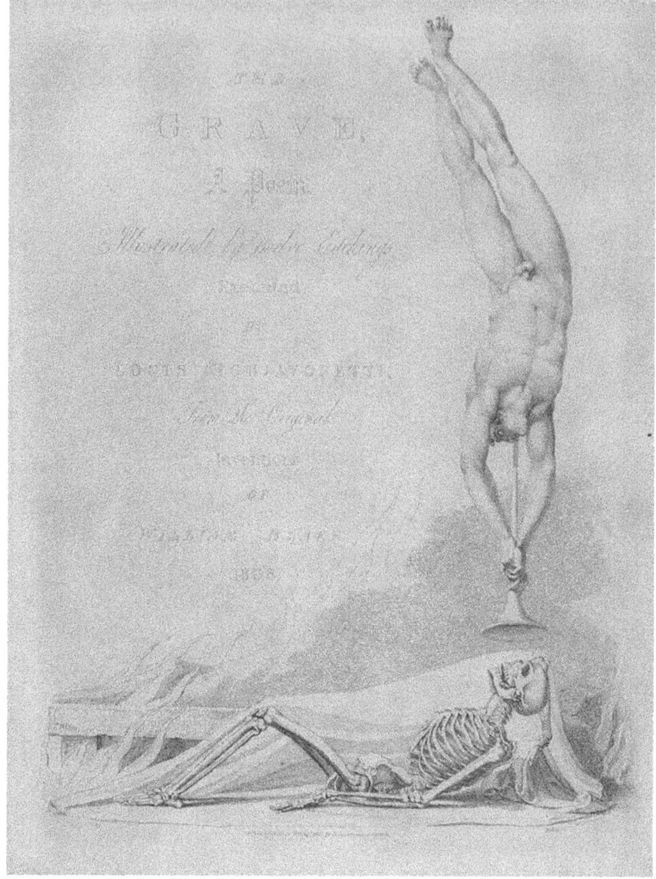

Figure 5 Title page from Robert Blair, *The Grave* (1808). Engraved by Luigi Schiavonetti from a design by William Blake. Photo courtesy Yale Center for British Art (Paul Mellon Collection).

issues at the centre of countercultural attention. What is more, this represents a paradigmatic instance of the amalgamation of Blake and surrealism for overtly political purposes; it bears all the hallmarks of an avant-garde intervention, albeit in a mass-circulation publication. Far from being treated as a cultural icon, the centre of venerated poetic and artistic traditions, Blake was being hijacked in the cause of social provocation.

This, in fact, is only one instance of Blake's countercultural currency. Without attempting to deal here with the huge question of his early 1960s literary reception, it was noted earlier that it was via Allen Ginsberg pre-eminently that Blake had entered the bloodstream of the British counterculture: the Albert Hall poetry event of 1965, in which Ginsberg performed, was a decisive rallying point. After this, invocations of Blake could be found everywhere in countercultural production, most audaciously in its graphics. One could cite numerous examples from both Britain and America. The obscure American underground press magazine *Strange*, for instance, would use exactly the same appropriated image by Blake that Martin Sharp had plundered from Ernst, and place it on the cover of its special 'Blake Power' issue (no. 5) of 1971. This testifies to the way that Blakean imagery was circulated and repurposed. Back in Britain, *International Times* would make regular allusions to Blake. Sometimes, it indulged a mystical view of Blake, in relation to ancient British traditions, that owed something to Blake scholars such as Kathleen Raine but more to popular writers on prehistoric antiquity such as John Michell. Hence, in issue 111 of 1971 we find an article on 'William Blake and the Druids'. But more often, a politicised and anti-establishment Blake is presented: Blake as the scourge of conventionality, the critic of empire, of repressed sexuality, of joylessness. On the back cover of issue 59 of July 1969, in an issue which incorporated articles on Wilhelm Reich, R. D. Laing and William Burroughs, we read an incendiary proclamation from Blake: 'Art degraded, Imagination/ Denied, War Governs/ the Nations! Rouse Up,/ O Young Men/ of the New Age!/ Set your Foreheads Against/ the Ignorant Hirelings/ For we have Hirelings/ in the Camp & in the Court/ & in the University/ who Would, if they Could/ Forever Depress Mental/ and Prolong/ Corporeal War!'[31] Captioned simply 'Wm Blake', this in fact combines two separate sources: Blake's plate *Laocoön* contains the line 'Art Degraded Imagination Denied War Governed the Nations', while the remainder of the text comes from the prose section of Blake's 'Preface' to *Milton a Poem*.[32]

Two Blake scholars have been mentioned so far in this article: Jacob Bronowski, whose vision of Blake as respondent to the coming of industrialism to Britain influenced a machinist strand of British avant-gardism, and Kathleen Raine, whose sense of Blake's antique and esoteric sources suited the mystical vein of 1960s counterculture. But it was from two other scholarly readings of Blake that were influential in the mid-to-late 1960s – David Erdman's *Blake: Prophet Against Empire* of 1954, revised in 1969, and E. P. Thompson's *The Making of the English Working Class* of 1963 – that, aside from Ginsberg, the politicised countercultural understanding of the poet gained its main impetus. This is confirmed by a lengthy and sophisticated reading of Blake that was published in one of the later editions of *Oz*, published in the shadow of its then-ongoing trial in September 1971. I refer to what was ostensibly a review of the poet Adrian Mitchell's play, *Tyger*, published in *Oz*, no. 37, by David Widgery, a Marxist who would eventually become co-editor of the magazine.[33]

Widgery's article sadly suffered at the hand of the magazine's design team. It is almost unreadable, with the illustration from Blake's *Jerusalem* that has been overprinted onto it in psychedelic blues and pinks obscuring much of the text. As already mentioned, the piece was partly a response to Adrian Mitchell's play *Tyger*, which had been put on by the National Theatre in July 1971. As a good example of the enthusiasm for Blake among British poets of the period – particular aficionados included Michael Horovitz, editor of the *Children of Albion* anthology, as well as Mitchell – the play offered up an often-humorous image of an eccentric Blake beset by the misunderstandings and pomposities of his detractors. Transposed into the

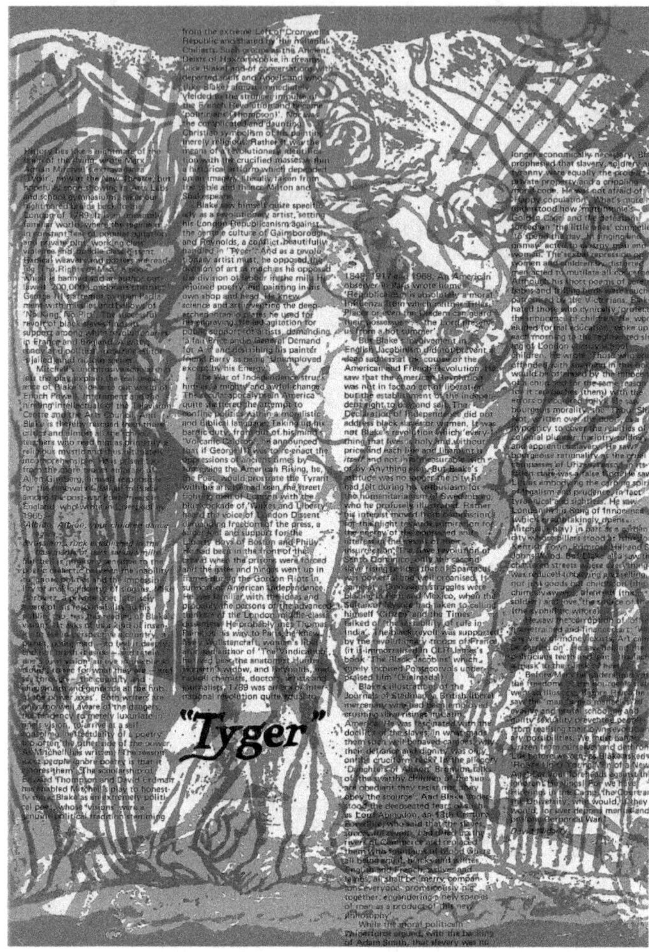

Figure 6 'Tyger', by David Widgery, *Oz* magazine, no. 37, September 1971, n.p. Private collection.

terms of the 1960s, Sir Joshua Reynolds, for instance, became Sir Joshua Rat. In an early scene, he read out the '27th of one hundred and forty discourses on Western Cutlery' (a satirical allusion on the part of Mitchell to Reynold's 'Discourses on Art' of 1797) on a pub TV, while Blake, sipping a pint of beer, muttered his derisive annotations.[34] Widgery approved of the play, which he hoped would soon be performed in school gymnasiums, but when it came down to it he offered little detailed explanation of its contents. His concerns were much wider, and to appreciate this some context is needed.

Some three years prior to this issue of *Oz*, in April 1968, Enoch Powell had delivered his notorious anti-immigration 'Rivers of Blood' speech in Birmingham, in which he had quoted Virgil's vision of the River Tiber 'foaming with blood' to alert fellow conservatives to the possible consequences of inter-racial mixing. Widgery was profoundly anti-racist: he would eventually be one of the organisers of the 'Rock Against Racism' movement of the mid-1970s. In line with *Oz*'s own committedly anti-racist stance (shown, for instance in the cover design for *Oz*, no. 23, as discussed earlier), he therefore used his *Tyger* review to reflect on issues of black oppression. Mitchell's play had itself included a lengthy section dealing with Blake's relationship with Captain John Gabriel Stedman, an officer in the Scots Brigade who had been sent to the Dutch colony of Surinam in South America to subdue a revolt by slaves against the owner of the plantation, and whose harrowing account of the treatment of slaves by their owners (*Narrative of a Five Years' Expedition against the Revolted Negroes of Surinam*, of 1796) Blake illustrated with a series of highly emotive engravings.[35] Widgery, however, used the play's emphasis on this episode as a springboard for a more scholarly appraisal of the anti-slavery views conveyed by Blake's imagery, drawing heavily on Erdman's recently republished *Blake: Prophet Against Empire*.[36] In Erdman's innovative reading of Blake's engravings, which included an account of British debates about slave-owning in the period, he settled at one point on a speech, in which the Tory Lord Abingdon had urged the abolitionist supporters of liberty and equality to consider the effects that their ideas had on stimulating the activities of slave mutineers in San Domingo: 'They have dried up the rivers of *commerce* and replaced them with "fountains of blood".'[37] Clearly, in earmarking this part of Erdman's analysis, Widgery was making parallels with Enoch Powell's scaremongering rhetoric of a few years earlier.

This provides an excellent example of how one of *Oz*'s more politicised writers mobilised Blake – or rather recent scholarly re-interpretations of him – to directly address 1960s countercultural ideology. Elsewehere in the same essay Widgery declared: 'Blake was not afraid of "Happy copulation". Moreover, he understood how "matrimonie's Golden Cage" and the defeatism forced on "the little ones" compelled "to spend the day, In singing [*sic*: sighing] and dismay" acted to destroy men and women.'[38] Before Wilhelm Reich, Widgery asserted, Blake 'saw the "man forged [*sic*: mind-forg'd] manacles" of evasive and brutal schooling and guilty sexuality prevented people from realising their own revolutionary possibilities'.[39] At the end of his article he quoted the same rousing lines from Blake's 'Preface' to *Milton* that had appeared two years earlier on the back cover of *International Times*.

All of this consolidates the sense that the pages of *Oz* produced a Blake who had pressing relevance for a young and politically astute late-1960s British audience, but it is significant that Blake was also mobilised in areas of the counterculture that considered both *Oz* and *International Times* far too close to establishment interests. King Mob, a situationist-inspired group, formed in 1968–69 around their low-grade, xerox-printed magazine *King Mob Echo*, saw the seductive *Oz* as too closely allied with the profit motive to dispense with pornographic titillation and weirdery. The Blake endorsed by King Mob was a political activist closely aligned with the avant-garde forebears favoured by the French situationists. These, once again, were mainly Dadaists and surrealists. In another cheaply produced magazine by a related formation of English situationists that preceded King Mob's publications – the short-lived *Rebel Worker* of 1966, edited by Charles Radcliffe – Blake was

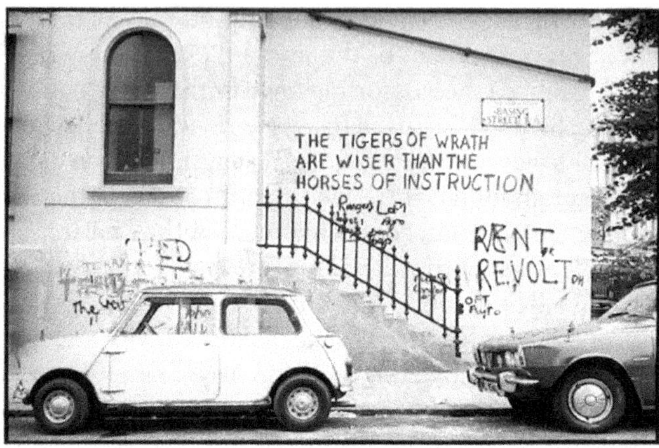

Figure 7 Photograph of graffiti by King Mob: Basing Street, London, 1968. Private collection.

given equivalent status to the heroes of French surrealism: Lautréamont, Charles Fourier and the Marquis de Sade. In a spirited text emphasising his links to the likes of William Godwin and Mary Wollstonecraft and lauding the 'prophetic surreality of his visions', the anonymous author (Radcliffe?) was uncompromising in his condemnation of the 'bourgeoisification' of the English poet:

> The editions of his works printed by William Blake are highly-prized by cretinous bourgeois rare book collectors (let us spit in their faces and note in passing that everything he wrote spits in their faces too).[40]

However, King Mob went beyond this proto-punk stance and took to the streets with Blake. Their advocacy of his ideas came in the form of graffitied quotations from his writings, along with other slogans, scrawled on the walls of London buildings and then recorded photographically in flyers.[41] Blake was being appropriated in precisely the manner that the French situationists had made use of philosophical forebears in the streets of Paris just months earlier. The deployment by King Mob of Blake's famous aphorism at the expense of schoolmasters ('The Tygers of Wrath are Wiser than the Horses of Instruction') as one of their slogans might easily have been a distant echo of the Paris situationists' advocacy of Fourier, Blake's exact early nineteenth-century French contemporary in terms of the assertion of the rights of children in the face of repressive adult control.[42] As noted, Blake and Fourier had already been closely aligned in the pages of *Rebel Worker* magazine.[43]

King Mob's sympathies clearly lay with the proletarian struggle, and not with the middle-class liberal values that the group associated with *International Times* or *Oz*: they were deeply suspicious of hippies and more in sympathy with subcultural formations such as the Mods. But in the final analysis, their historical response to Blake was at one with the commercial wing of the 1960s underground. In all areas of countercultural publishing, Blake was wrested from high culture. His images and poems were cut away from their sources, decontextualised, repoliticised. Blake now spoke to issues of homosexual oppression, racism, sexual oppression, children's rights, women's liberation and stultifying state control.

To go back to the beginning of this discussion, it is striking how far the conception of Blake has travelled from the pastoralism of his 1930s neo-Romantic reception. But it is even more intriguing to reflect on how the late 1930s avant-garde Blake, synonymous with the coming of the machine, with mingled terror and awe at the new forms of energy unleashed in the industrial age – as glimpsed by Humphrey Jennings and consecrated in Paolozzi's 'Newton' statue outside the British Library – seems at odds with the figure of the rebellious Blake of the counterculture. Equally, Bacon's 'high art' response to Blake seems like an isolated gesture in a rapidly shifting cultural landscape. The Blake of countercultural interest represents a further stage of the avant-garde's assimilation of the art of the past in the search for new social relevance. By the late 1960s, it might be argued, Blake was seen less as a respondent to the technological and material forces of the modern age, and more as someone in tune with the critique of what Herbert Marcuse, one of the leading ideologues of the counterculture, saw as the 'advanced industrial-technical complex' of the West.[44] Just as the British counterculture itself, in its brief flowering in the late 1960s and early 1970s, attempted a sublation of cultural practices of various kinds into the praxis of life, so Blake was now pressed into the service of the multiple causes of 1960s political activism. This was Blake at his most avant-garde.

In memory of Trevor and Anthony Hopkins.

Notes

1 For a discussion of the latter tendency see David Hopkins, 'William Blake and British Surrealism: Humphrey Jennings, the Impact of Machines and the Case for Dada', *Visual Culture in Britain*, 19 (2018), 305–20.

2 *Children of Albion: Poetry of the 'Underground' in Britain*, ed. M. Horovitz (Penguin Books, Harmondsworth, 1969).

3 In his *Theory of the Avant-Garde* (translated by Michael Shaw, Minneapolis: University of Minnesota, 1984), Peter Bürger uses Dada, futurism, surrealism and the left avant-garde in Russia and Germany as his touchstones. When it comes to surrealism, its techniques, particularly 'automatic writing', are seen as exemplifications of the characteristic avant-garde concern with montage in opposition to the 'organic' work of art. See Bürger, *Theory of the Avant-Garde*, pp. 79–80.

4 *Ibid.*, p. 22.

5 *Ibid.*, p. 49.

6 For an account of the surrealist movement's dialogue with communism see H. Lewis, *Dada Turns Red: The Politics of Surrealism* (Edinburgh: Edinburgh University Press, 1988).

7 *Ibid.*, pp. 97–139.

8 In an influential reconsideration of Bürger's theories, Hal Foster is particularly critical of the overly simplistic linkage of 'art' and 'life' in Bürger: see Hal Foster, 'Who's Afraid of the Neo-Avant-Garde', in his *The Return of the Real* (Cambridge, MA and London: MIT Press, 1996), pp. 15–17. Although Foster concedes that the neo-avant-garde often settled too easily for a 'reconnection of art and life' (as in Pop Art), his article is important for its wholesale critique of the limitations of Bürger's theory.

9 For discussion of Nash in relation to Blake see, for instance, A. Causey, *Paul Nash* (Oxford: Clarendon Press, 1980), p. 9.

10 See David Hopkins, 'William Blake and British Surrealism: Humphrey Jennings, the Impact of Machines and the Case for Dada', *Visual Culture In Britain*, 19 (2018), 305–20.

11 See National Portrait Gallery, London, extended cataloge entry 1809: James Deville, 'William Blake (1823)', www.npg.org.uk (accessed 10 March 2021).

12 Blake's wife Catherine had apparently felt that the cast misrepresented her husband. See the discussion of Bacon's response to the cast in M. Stevens and A. Swan, *Francis Bacon: Revelations* (London: Collins, 2021), pp. 381–2.

13 Much of this information derives from M. Harrison, *Francis Bacon: Photography, Film and the Practice of Painting* (London: Thames & Hudson, 2005), pp. 133–4.

14 Bacon in M. Archimbaud, *Francis Bacon in Conversation with Michel Archimbaud* (London: Phaidon, 1993), p. 121.

15 J. Jones, 'Study for Portrait II: After the Life Mask of Willam Blake, Francis Bacon (1955)', *Guardian* (23 February 2002), www.theguardian.com/culture/2002/feb/23/art.williamblake (accessed 1 February 2021).

16 M. Cappock, *Francis Bacon's Studio* (London and New York: Merrell, 2005), p. 108.

17 *Ibid.*, p. 109.

18 For discussion of Miró's debt to Blake, see D. Lomas, *The Haunted Self: Surrealism: Psychoanalysis: Subjectivity* (New Haven and London: Yale University Press, 2000), pp. 189–90.

19 The classic early texts on this process are R. Williams, *Culture and Society 1780–1950* (London: Chatto & Windus, 1958), and *Keywords: A Vocabulary of Culture and Society* (London: Fontana, 1976). The latter helped redefine terms such as 'culture' and 'class' in the context of the mid-1970s. Other seminal studies include R. Hoggart, *The Uses of Literacy* (London: Chatto & Windus, 1957).

20 Adorno and Horkheimer discuss the concept of the 'culture industry' in *Dialektik der Aufklärung* (Amsterdam: Querido Verlag, 1947.)

21 J. Clarke, S. Hall, T. Jefferson and B. Roberts, 'Subcultures, Cultures and Class', in S. Hall and T. Jefferson (eds), *Resistance through Rituals: Youth Subcultures in Post-War Britain* (London and New York: Routledge, 2nd edn, 2006), p. 6; originally published in *Working Papers in Cultural Studies*, 7/8 (1975).

22 *Ibid.*, pp. 6–7.

23 Little work on Blake and British counterculture has been done to date. For his American countercultural reception, see S. F. Eisenman (ed.), *William Blake and the Age of Aquarius* (Evanston, ILL and Princeton, NJ: Northwestern University (Block Museum of Art) and Princeton University Press, 2017).

24 P. Stansill and D. Mairowitz (eds), *BAMN (By Any Means Necessary): Outlaw Manifestos and Ephemera, 1965–70* (Harmondsworth: Penguin, 1971), p. 13.

25 A. Wilson: 'Spontaneous Underground: An Introduction to London's Psychedelic Scenes, 1965–1968', in C. Grunenberg and J. Harris (eds), *Summer of Love: Psychedelic Art, Social Crisis and Counterculture in the 1960s* (Liverpool: Liverpool University Press, 2005), p. 91.

26 For an interesting study of the relationship between visual culture studies and art historical approaches, see M. Dikovitskaya (ed.), *Visual Culture: The Study of the Visual after the Cultural Turn* (Cambridge, MA and London: MIT Press, 2006).

27 *Oz*, 23 (August/September 1969), p. 9.

28 *Ibid.*, p. 17.

29 *Ibid.*, pp. 5, 20, 24–5.

30 *Ibid.*, p. 5: reproduction of Max Ernst's collage from *La Femme 100 Têtes:* 'A crime or a miracle: a complete human being'.

31 *International Times*, 59 (July 1969), back cover.

32 The line from Blake's engraving of the Laocoön can be found at the very base of the engraving. For a useful discussion of it, as well as the rest of the annotations Blake added to the engraving, see Irene Taylor, 'Blake's Laocoön', in *Blake: An Illustrated Quarterly*, vol 10, issue 3 (Winter 1976–77), 73 and passim. For the 'Preface' to Milton a Poem' see *William Blake: The Complete Poems*, ed. Alicia Ostriker (Harmondsworth: Penguin, 1977, reprinted 2004), p. 513.

33 D. Widgery, 'Tyger', *Oz*, 37 (September 1971), n.p.

34 See A. Mitchell, *Tyger: A Celebration Based on the Life and Work of William Blake* (London: Jonathan Cape, 1971), pp. 15–17. Reynolds's 'Discourses', which were originally delivered at the Royal Academy, London between 1761 and 1791, and represented a statement of classical precepts regarding painting and sculpture, appeared together in a single volume in 1797. Blake's famous 'annotations' to Reynolds, repudiating the academician's tone of address as well as his principles, were a series of marginal notes incorporated into Blake's copy of the three-volume edition of Reynolds's writings published in 1798.

35 See Mitchell, *Tyger*, pp. 49–55.

36 D. Erdman, *Blake: Prophet Against Empire* (Princeton, NJ: Princeton University Press, 1969); first published 1954.

37 *Ibid.*, p. 238.

38 D. Widgery, 'Tyger', *Oz*, 37 (September 1971), n.p.

39 *Ibid.*

40 C. Radcliffe [?], 'BLAKE', *Rebel Worker*, 6 (1966), 10.

41 See the English Section of the Situationist International, *King Mob Echo* (reprint) (Edinburgh: Dark Star, 2000), pp. 89–101.

42 For this photograph see *Ibid.*, p. 96.

43 *Ibid.*, pp. 9–10. For an account of Fourier's ideas regarding childhood and play, see David Hopkins, *Dark Toys: Surrealism and the Culture of Childhood* (New Haven and London: Yale University Press, 2021), pp. 201–7.

44 Herbert Marcuse, *One Dimensional Man* (London: Routledge & Kegan Paul, 1964).

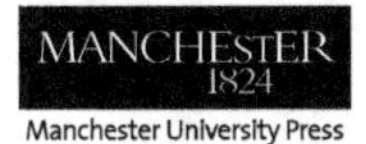

Iain Sinclair, William Blake and the Visionary Poetry of the 1960s

JAMES RILEY, UNIVERSITY OF CAMBRIDGE

Abstract

This article considers the use made of William Blake by a range of writers associated with the 'countercultural' milieu of the 1960s, particularly those linked to its London-based literary context. Iain Sinclair is offered as a writer who, in his appreciation of Blake, stands apart from the poets linked to the anthology, *Children of Albion* (1969). The article unpacks this distinction, analysing Sinclair's 'topographic' take in comparison to the 'visionary' mode of his contemporaries. Having established this dualism, the argument then questions the nature of the visionary poetics assumed to apply to the likes of key poets from the era. The work of Michael Horovitz is brought into view, as is that of Harry Fainlight. In essence, these multiple discourses point to the plurality of Blake as a figure of influence and the variation underpinning his literary utility in post-1960s poetry.

Keywords: 1960s; counterculture; visionary; poetry; topography; Sinclair; Horovitz; Fainlight

'I arrive at my argument's central principle', writes Harold Bloom, famously, in *The Anxiety of Influence* (1973), when imagining the oedipal struggle between 'two strong, authentic poets'. Poetic influence, Bloom contends, 'always proceeds by a misreading of the prior poet, an act of creative correction that is actually and necessarily a misinterpretation'. Not content with such a sweeping gesture, Bloom then expands out to a much wider, generalised analysis of 'Western poetry since the Renaissance'. In Bloom's view, this macro-history reveals a dynamic of anxiety and 'self-saving caricature', a process of 'distortion, of perverse, wilful revisionism' which in turn feeds into subsequent modalities. Indeed, without this intentional interplay, he argues, 'modern poetry as such could not exist'.[1]

The familiarity of this argument has now rendered it somewhat obvious. The interpretative radicalism of *The Anxiety of Influence* – in a realisation of its argumentative intention – has given rise to a truism regarding influence, that 'originality' is built on creative engagements with a wider frame of literary reference, conscious or not. However, Bloom's use of the psychologically inflected 'anxiety' belies the material mechanism of textual production. It is not exceptional that poets should 'struggle' with their urtexts. Whether 'strong' or not, beyond the aggrandising mysticism of Bloom's evaluation, there remains the practice of writing – an ongoing process powered by an engine of citation, modification, intertextuality and dissemination. T. S. Eliot had a better and more accurate take on this 'frightful toil' in 'The Function of Criticism' (1923) when he described literary composition as, for the most part, 'critical labour; the labour of sifting, combining, constructing, expunging, correcting, testing'.[2] Not so much anxiety, then, as mediation, manufacture and the work of thought.

Bulletin of the John Rylands Library, Volume 98, No. 1 (Spring 2022), pp. 75–92, published by Manchester University Press.
http://dx.doi.org/10.7227/BJRL.98.1.7

The terms of Bloom's argument are suited to two of his literary exemplars, John Milton and William Blake. It is Blake's engagement with Milton that Bloom cites just prior to the announcement of his 'central principle'. He offers Blake as 'the most profound and original theorist of revisionism to appear since the Enlightenment', noting that for Blake, 'to be enslaved by any precursor's system is to inhibit creativity by an obsessive reasoning and comparing'. However, Bloom adds that Blake was not immune from this 'disease of self-consciousness', with his work variously celebrating and wrestling with the weight of his predecessor's achievements.[3] In *Milton a Poem* (1804–10), Blake confronts this influence, filling 'Milton's Shadow' with an array of 'Dragon Forms'.[4] Bloom reads this as Blake cataloguing the 'litany of evils' that 'came to him most powerfully' in his 'vision of the greatest of his predecessors'.[5] It is an admission that he writes within Milton's shadow while at the same time attempting to move beyond its range. The implied overshadowing is overwhelming in its connotations, but Blake is here acknowledging it, containing it, putting it to work in his own poetic act.

Summarising the interplay in 2008, Bloom put it that 'the strongest influence Blake ever knew was that of John Milton, as compounded with the Bible'. He added that 'of all literary texts Milton and the Bible most 'possessed' Blake, though Shakespeare and Dante also had a strong influence upon him'.[6] The language again reiterates Bloom's critical preoccupation, the idea of a 'strong' influence felt between correspondingly 'strong' poets; literary productivity thus rendered as a trans-historic heroic struggle, metatextually reflective of the conflicts that echo through both *Milton* and *Paradise Lost* (1667). Worthy of note beyond Bloom's mythologising critical schema is the additional phrase 'possessed'. Indicative not just of influence but also 'inspiration' (in the sense of *inspirare*, 'to breathe into'), 'possessed' initially works to encapsulate Blake's preoccupation with Milton. However, this sense of enthusiasm gives way to another dynamic, one that covertly undercuts the 'misprision' or misinterpretation that Bloom uses as the basis of his take on anxiety.[7] When the proprietorial implication of 'possessed' is brought into play alongside the further sense of spiritual, if not demonic possession, the active creativity of one poet's engagement with the other recedes into a sense of passivity. Possession, the occult process of one entity stepping into and speaking through another, is suggestive of a reduction rather than an amplification of agency. In the above comment it seems that it is not Blake who possesses a material text – an object that variously carries the names of the Bible, Dante, Shakespeare and Milton – but that these writers exert a pull and a hold over him, to the extent that 'William Blake' is implicitly re-figured as something of a vessel. Bloom's word choice does not yield an image of the great revisionist, but a figure ventriloquised by the voices of the past which remain active within his contemporaneous sphere of reading.

A similar framing is present when Blake is considered as a figure of Miltonic stature, a point of significant influence upon those writers who follow him. In *Blake and Modern Literature* (2006), for example, Edward Larrissy attempts 'to offer an account of Blake's afterlife which shows that he was central in the retrospective construction of Romanticism that was acceptable to the twentieth century', adding that 'he assisted in the gestation of innovative writing in the modern period'.[8] There is little to disagree with here. Note, however, the quietly ghostly implications of 'afterlife'. Granted, this is a widespread critical shorthand used to allude to matters of reception and legacy. In this instance, though, when coupled with the personal 'he' there is an additional sense created of Blake as an active presence. The language used creates an image not just of Blake's writing and its transmission, but of Blake himself as a virtual spirit guide, centrally orchestrating the work that follows his own.

I draw attention to these turns of phrase because of their role within claims regarding 'modern poetry', particularly within Bloom's theory of anxiety. As indicated, he posits that inter-generational 'corrective creation' and associated processes within the framework constitute a precondition for modern poetry, the genetic history upon which it depends. My contention here is that the post-Blakean lineage within the modern sphere follows a different trajectory of influence, one based upon explicit self-consciousness rather than a sensibility akin to anxiety; that is to say, within the post-1945 period and onwards to the contemporary, one finds Blake appearing across a range of media with the type of distinct, centralised presence alluded to in Larrissy's language. This material does evince a 'caricature' and in some cases a 'wilful revisionism' – as Bloom would put it – but one also finds a level of poetic invocation, a wilful desire to be 'possessed'; this is explicitly inspired, historically legitimised by and placed into virtual communion with William Blake. Here 'William Blake' signifies less a point of textual or intertextual reference, and more of a catalysing presence: a name to be conjured when the matter of influence comes to the fore.

A case in point is the work of Allen Ginsberg. In 1948, in a moment that has since become iconic in the cultural history of the Beat Generation, Ginsberg 'heard' the 'very deep earthen grave voice' of Blake while reclining on the bed in his East Harlem apartment.[9] As he recounted to Tom Clark in 1965, Ginsberg had been reading *Songs of Innocence and of Experience* (1794) when the voice began. 'Blake' continued to recite from the volume and Ginsberg found himself listening to 'Ah Sun-flower', 'The Sick Rose' and 'The Little Girl Lost'. Reflecting on the 'apparitional voice, in the room' Ginsberg described how it enhanced his interpretative engagement with the text, it 'woke me further deep in my understanding of the poem'.[10] From here, the encounter segued into an epiphanic, initiatory experience whereby Ginsberg fully apprehended the work and his role within it: 'I suddenly realised that *this* existence was *it*! And, that I was born in order to experience up to this very moment.'[11] As James Campbell later put it, 'the voice of Blake became the voice of God, and – like many seers of visions before him – Ginsberg had no doubt that God was speaking directly to him and about him'.[12] To use Aldous Huxley's distinction from *Heaven and Hell* (1956), whether the paranormality of Ginsberg's 'auditory hallucination' is accepted or not, he describes a 'visionary' experience. Where a 'mystical' experience goes 'beyond the realm of opposites', visionary experience is 'still in that realm'.[13] Accordingly, Ginsberg does not conceive of an apotheosis with Blake. As he describes it, his reception of the poet's voice serves rather to elevate and spiritualise his view of the world around him.

As his account continues and he wanders round the campus of New York's Columbia University and its bookshop, Ginsberg finds that the books on sale are still books and the store assistant is still the store assistant. He has not transcended the material world, nor does he conceive of a cosmology as complex as that in Blake's own poetry. Instead, Ginsberg gains a sense of the potential carried by the books he sees and in those he encounters. Everyone, he claims, knows the 'truth', but only Ginsberg is able to acknowledge it. In narrating these events to Clark in the mid-1960s, Ginsberg was echoing aspects of the wider visionary tradition from Percy Shelley's acknowledgement of poets as 'hierophants of unapprehended inspiration' to Arthur Rimbaud's insistence on a 'systematised disorganisation of the senses' as well as Charles Olson's discussion of poetry as affective energy in 'Projective Verse' (1950).[14] Overall, Ginsberg's experience furnished him with (or at least allowed him to conceptualise) what might be termed an occult sensibility: an awareness of knowledge or power which lies hidden or is otherwise obscured.

One finds a similar dynamic operating in a range of subsequent multimedia works that variously invoke Blake and his writing. In his epic, esoteric poem *Vale Royal* (1995), Aidan Andrew Dun draws on the persona of Blake and Thomas Chatterton to plot a performative quest through the urban wastelands of London's King's Cross.[15] In *Public House* (2015), her impressionistic portrait of the Ivy House pub in Peckham, filmmaker Sarah Turner alludes via a group performance to Blake's childhood visions of 'a tree filled with angels' on Peckham Rye when encapsulating the deep historical value of the community space she documents.[16] Meanwhile, between these examples one finds parallel evocations such as the song 'History' (1995) by The Verve, in which Wigan-born singer Richard Ashcroft creates a bleak atmosphere of urban alienation by blending his own lyrics with those of Blake's 'London' (1794).[17] In each case, as with Ginsberg's writing, the engagement with the Blakean corpus is not purely citational. Extending across multiple platforms, these texts play with the visionary aura of Blake and his associations. In essence, Blake's explicit influence is amplified as a means to legitimise the projects in question. With this spiritual guide leading the way, the texts position themselves as part of an illustrious lineage and, in turn, their authors are able to cultivate a particular perspective of their urban locations, primarily London and New York. In other words, writing in deference to Blake afforded these practitioners the privilege of vision, the discourse necessary to assume a spiritualised view of their surroundings; one which, like Ginsberg's view of New York, carries untapped potential just beneath the everyday surface.

This is a position of exceptionalism, in which the poet takes the role of seer: in the world but at the same time standing outside it. Giorgio Agamben would call it the condition of the contemporary, the ambiguous vantage point occupied by those 'who neither perfectly coincide with [their time] nor adjust themselves to its demands'.[18] Michael Horovitz neatly encapsulates this subjectivity in 'Spring Welcomes you to London' (1965). Radiating with '7 a.m. Sunday sunshine', the poem offers a vignette of an encounter between three symbolic figures: an exuberant poet, a man in a 'shooting-brake' removing pigeons from the Soho street, and a curious, if not suspicious, policeman.[19] Horovitz adds an asterisk to his first use of 'pigeon' which directs readers to a footnote equating the birds with 'penguins' as in the famous logo of Penguin Books. Penguin would go on to publish Horovitz's anthology *Children of Albion: Poetry of the Underground in Britain* (1969) and the company had, since 1962, regularly issued the Penguin Modern Poets series which, by 1965, had featured the likes of Ginsberg, Gregory Corso and Lawrence Ferlinghetti.[20] It is thus easy to follow Horovitz's connotation and interpret the graphic 'penguin' as a marker of literary expression. With this analogy in place, the text becomes a tussle between poetry understood as a form of unfettered freedom ('delivered by wings from petty civic fogs') and stereotypical forces of the 'establishment'. The latter 'loom' in, 'hatchet-faced', and with 'bye-laws' attempt to limit the free-flowing activity symbolised by the free movement of the birds.[21] The speaker, 'up and about' in the dawn, outside 'normal' working hours and at odds with those variously 'policing' the streets, is in sympathy with the 'doves pigeons robins sparrows'.[22] Such an alignment suggests that for Horovitz, the poet is to be afforded the same liberty to engage, unhindered, in flights of fancy.

With 'Spring Welcomes You to London', Horovitz was voicing a classic trope of the 1960s, that of a stance of recalcitrant opposition towards authority. Ginsberg's Blake experience has been read in a similar manner. Campbell reflects that this 'unique communion' foregrounded the distance between Ginsberg's intense engagement with poetry and that of his professors at Columbia, Mark Van Doren and Lionel Trilling, 'propounders of the academic approach to literature and [...] the academic approach to life, keeper-downers, suppressors of the gospel that literature really contained'.[23] Much the same could be said for Dun and Turner. Their Blakean invocations fed into close, lyrical engagements with the city, operating as shorthand for a generalised critique of gentrification and its economically oriented erasure of history and locality. As for Ashcroft, co-opting 'London' into 'History' adds gravitas to the persona cultivated elsewhere in his lyrics, that of a self-mythologising urban outsider. Speaking with and through the voice of Blake, these re-imaginings offer consistently resistant gestures. In Bloom's schema, by contrast, the inheritances of Blake along with their associated recalibrations ultimately feed into the construction of the western canon. It is this sense of cultural conservatism that Ginsberg and Horovitz *et al.* write against. Their Blake is a disruptive and unquiet spirit. That there should be plural lines of influence and adaptation extending out from a poetic corpus, especially one as rich and as varied as that of William Blake, is not surprising. However, given the contingency that Bloom identifies between his designated figures of influence and 'modern poetry as such', the seemingly dissonant use made of Blake indicated here invites reflection – not least because to analyse the poet's reception via 'modern' literary practice also provides a means to understand the 'visionary' mode within the same milieu.

To consider the modus operandi underpinning the use made of Blake by 'modern poetry', it is useful to refer to the work of a writer who holds Blake in similarly high regard. Shadowing each of the authors mentioned thus far, with a particular investment in the culture of the 1960s, is the writer, poet and filmmaker, Iain Sinclair. In 2007, Sinclair delivered a lecture at London's Swedenborg Society which was published in 2012 as the short book *Blake's London: The Topographic Sublime.* Over the course of this typically wide-ranging blend of interpretation, autobiography and imaginative cartography, Sinclair described the formative influence of William Blake upon his long-term, long-form work of metropolitan psychogeography. In the book, Sinclair talks about buying Geoffrey Keynes's 1966 edition of *Blake: Complete Writings* from London's Compendium Bookshop in 1971, a volume that became his '*I Ching*, an almanac of divination'.[24] Moving further back into a personal chronology, Sinclair describes returning to London in 1967 after film school in Dublin and noticing that 'Blake was being recognised as a significant figure' among the writers of the city's poetry network.[25] As he describes it, this was not so much a phase of critical re-evaluation as a period of creative engagement, a moment defined by the appropriation of Blake rather than his re-citation:

> That 1960s counterculture found qualities in Blake to which they instinctively responded. They re-invented him in their own image. He was pressed into the charivari of the *International Times* alongside William Burroughs, Wilhelm Reich and Michael Moorcock's Jerry Cornelius.[26]

In terms of the '1960s counterculture', then, the apostrophe in *Blake's London* does not work as part of a historical comparison. Sinclair is not considering the 1960s from the perspective of the eighteenth century or vice versa. Instead, he evokes an act of speculative invocation, and describes a shared artistic territory onto which a set of writers converge.

Blake's London continues with Sinclair recalling his London-based encounter with Allen Ginsberg for his film documentary on the poet, *Ah Sunflower!* (1967). Having mentioned Ginsberg's own New York vision of Blake in 1948, Sinclair continues:

> When I was filming Ginsberg, the place that he wanted to visit was the top of Primrose Hill. And we went to the top of Primrose Hill. We filmed interviews with him there, and he read poems. [...] We felt, as we set up the camera, that Ginsberg was trying to raise the spirit of Blake over the city again from this vantage point.[27]

Aware that 'this vantage point', Primrose Hill, was a site of 'great spiritual significance' for Blake, the place where he claimed to have seen 'the spiritual Sun', Sinclair presents Ginsberg's in-situ reading as a point of linkage between the two visionary poets.[28] In his recall it is a moment of attempted conjuration, of hailing, a point of trans-historical feedback from a receiver to the sender, one that also serves to reiterate its locality as a zone of sacred space, hence the importance for Sinclair. He offers his entanglement within the lattice of poetry and place that constitutes 'London's dreaming' as his own point of ignition: 'that's where it started for me, the 60s sense of Blake, the sense of privileged topography'.[29]

From *Lud Heat* (1975) to the more recent elegy *The Last London* (2017), Sinclair's brief but precise summation seems to make sense as regards the work that followed *Ah Sunflower!* As a writer informed by the British and American countercultures of the 1960s, whose work maps the hidden and erased contours of the city with a heightened, almost hallucinatory intensity, Sinclair initially seems like the consummate Neo-Blakean author. That said, earlier in *Blake's London*, Sinclair makes a distinction between these terms of definition. As the text develops, what Sinclair terms 'the 60s sense of Blake' starts to drift away from his primary point of interest in the poet's work, 'the sense of privileged topography'. It is as if the delineation of his own point of departure actually marks out a crossroads within the Blakean revival outlined. While 'the 60s sense of Blake' goes in one direction, Sinclair suggests that his project goes in another; it is a movement with Blake as 'a presence, a guide, an advocate' towards 'privileged topography' and specifically the topography of London. While Ginsberg goes from his interview with Sinclair on Primrose Hill to the border country to write 'Wales: A Visitation' (1967), a poem that reverberates with 'the cry of Blake', Sinclair describes himself doubling down into the urban zone.[30] Here, his Limehouse and Hawksmoor excursions are remembered as the pursuit of 'a figure, a sleeping giant', a 'self-forged daemon' that equates not to 'humankind' or to 'Britain' but belongs, unequivocally, 'to the ground of London'.[31] As a retrospective statement of artistic intent, then, Sinclair uses *Blake's London* to suggest that his reading of the poet's work and the project it inspires is different to, if not in tension with, the reception of Blake on the part of the (broadly defined) 1960s counterculture. As Sinclair puts it, what he saw in the charivari of the *International Times* was 'not the topographer Blake' but the Blake of *Glad Day*.[32]

Glad Day, also known as *Albion Rose* and *The Dance of Albion*, is an engraving made by Blake circa 1795, based on an earlier drawing, that speaks of energy and liberation. It adorns the cover of Horovitz's *Children of Albion*, and Sinclair seems to be invoking this volume when using the image to emblematise 'the 60s sense of Blake'. An epiphanic centrifuge of spiritual sun, *Glad Day* is distinctly celebratory. It is an image of unfettered existence that is aspirant, utopian and apocalyptic – apocalyptic in the sense of revealing – and one which communicates a distinct sense of jubilation. Whether, as Peter Ackroyd speculates, it is an image that Blake originally made as a drawing to mark the end of his arduous apprenticeship or whether it is a projective 'recognition of his own great powers', *Glad Day* is a clarion call to step out of the day-to-day into a higher state of being.[33] In this regard, it sits well with the work and ideas of the symbolic figures Sinclair invokes as part of the countercultural parade: William Burroughs, Wilhelm Reich and Jerry Cornelius.

Burroughs, Reich and Cornelius are not unconnected, but are ostensibly figures linked to very separate spheres: an experimental novelist, a radical psychoanalyst and a fictional character. However, their representative texts such as Burroughs's *Nova Express* (1964), Reich's *The Function of the Orgasm* (1927) and Moorcock's first Cornelius novel, *The Final Programme* (1969), circulated at the same time in 1960s London and share a liberative and emancipatory trajectory. *Nova Express*, one of Burroughs's cut-up texts, spoke of breaking through into the 'Grey Room', storming the reality studio and punching a hole in reality; Reich wished to accumulate the manifold energies of the orgasmic state as a conduit to socio-economic change; and Cornelius – Moorcock's generation-spanning, identity-shifting trickster figure – is a man unbound by the rules of time that elsewhere govern the horizon of the quotidian.[34] Taken together, the proposed lineage that runs from *Glad Day* to *The Final Programme* aligns the counterculture with an escapist, transcendental project. Such a reading reflects the tone of the countercultural 'branding', as it were, of the time. Writing in 'Youth and the Great Refusal', a March 1968 article for *The Nation*, the American sociologist Theodore Roszak described the countercultural impetus as:

> the effort to discover new types of community, new family patterns, new sexual mores, new kinds of livelihood, new aesthetic forms, new personal identities on the far side of power politics, the bourgeois home, and the Protestant work ethic.[35]

Writing in 1969, Joseph Berke made a similar point, describing the counterculture as a wave of youth-led, politically orientated attempts to move away from 'the parental stem'.[36] Although somewhat decontextualised, *Glad Day* works as a neat symbol of these sentiments. It is an emblem of the power of youth; one that speaks of a radicalised sense of 'the new' as well as a new dawn rising, a kind of dynamic, libidinal departure from past forms and behaviours.

By contrast, when describing his creative link to Blake, Sinclair is little concerned with images that encapsulate a certain group identity or project of the 1960s. He speaks instead of his own, singular navigation of the text and discusses how it informed his singular take on the city. That is to say, Sinclair focuses his attention on *Jerusalem The Emanation of the Giant Albion* (1804–20) not in terms of the apotheosis suggested by the thrust of its 'prophetic' narrative, but in terms of the instructions it offers for what he calls 'a particular kind of walk … an eccentric journey both spiritual and physical'.[37] According to Sinclair, the sequence that he '[came] back to time and time again' can be found in the second chapter of *Jerusalem*: the narration of Los's descent into the interior of fallen Albion. It is a carefully mapped excursion through east London, 'that part beyond the tower', a zone which at the time of the poem's composition, Sinclair reminds us, was 'well off the official charts':[38]

> He came down from Highgate thro Hackney & Holloway towards London
> Till he came to old Stratford & thence to Stepney & the Isle
> Of Leuthas Dogs, thence thro the narrows of the Rivers side
> And saw every minute particular, the jewels of Albion, running down
> The kennels of the streets & lanes as if they were abhorrd.
> Every Universal Form, was become barren mountains of Moral
> Virtue: and every Minute Particular hardend into grains of sand:
> And all the tendernesses of the soul cast forth as filth & mire,
> Among the winding places of deep contemplation intricate
> To where the Tower of London frownd dreadful over Jerusalem:
> A building of Luvah builded in Jerusalems eastern gate to be

> His secluded Court: thence to Bethlehem where was builded
> Dens of despair in the house of bread: enquiring in vain
> Of stones and rocks he took his way, for human form was none:
> And thus he spoke, looking on Albions City with many tears.[39]

It is the notion of a spiritual and physical journey, an inward and outward movement, that is of interest to Sinclair here. Blake has Albion extend into the fabric of the city, and this is an imagined fibrillation that mirrors something of the poet's own embodied experience of London. 'London physically affects him', notes Sinclair when describing the 'torment of the stomach' Blake often felt after wandering across 'Hampstead, Highgate, Hornsey, Muswell Hill'.[40]

For Sinclair, the value of this 'imprint' on the psychic chart of London, as well as the geographic specificity of poems like *Jerusalem*, is that they work as maps of the city's future development. 'Blake's lines spike the energy points', says Sinclair, 'the litany of his mental journey is like acupuncture'.[41] *Jerusalem* assumes such paradigmatic importance for Sinclair because it prefigured what he was trying to do in *Lud Heat* and subsequent texts. Reading and re-reading the poem while working as a groundskeeper in the churchyards of East London, Sinclair was furnished with a heightened register, the tools of 'ambulant sign-making', that allowed him to conceptualise the city's architectural, mythic and economic potency as well as its change from buried giant to consuming leviathan.[42]

His, then, is a visionary project but one that focuses on the ground below rather than the world beyond. In this respect, one could argue that Sinclair looks slightly askance at the conceptualisation of 'vision' that one might more typically associate with the countercultural milieu. Writing in 'The Menacing Eye' (1968), an essay that appeared in the *International Times* in January 1968, Jeff Nuttall describes the swirl of language surrounding the use and understanding of 'psychedelics'. He talks about 'transcendence, hallucination, mind expansion and fantasy', arguing that they are essentially synonyms for 'vision', what he calls 'the artistic imperative that provides a glimpse through the passive/utilitarian barrier of perception to a wider, therefore more complete awareness'.[43] Here, Nuttall is alluding to Blake's much cited line from *The Marriage of Heaven and Hell* (1791) regarding the doors of perception and the appearance of the 'infinite'.[44] At the same time, he echoes Huxley's appropriation of Blake for the title of his mescaline essay *The Doors of Perception* (1954). Huxley writes at length about the visual effects of the drug, noting that while it does not yield entry to the type of 'inner world described by Blake', it produces a vast sharpening of the sensorium. The 'other world' opened by mescaline remains that 'out there' which can be seen 'with the eyes open', but it appears newly unveiled, imbued with a hitherto unknown vividness. As Huxley puts it, 'I was seeing what Adam had seen on the morning on his creation.'[45] Sinclair's archaeological, often associatively encyclopaedic approach to the capital is an 'artistic imperative' that is comparable in terms of its intention to foreground a previously hidden London. The emphasis, as he puts it in *Lights Out for the Territory* (1997), is on the matter of the city: a search for a psychogeographic communion or act of speculative mediumship in which writing and walking fuse in order to invoke 'dormant energies'. As Sinclair explains at the start of *Lights Out*:

> The notion was to cut a crude V into the sprawl of the city … (I had developed this curious conceit while working on my novel *Radon Daughters*: that the physical movements of the characters across their territory might spell out the letters of a secret alphabet. Dynamic shapes, with ambitions to achieve a life of their own, quite independent of their supposed author. These botched runes, burnt into the script in the heat of creation, offer an alternative reading – a subterranean, preconscious text capable of divination and prophecy. A sorcerer's grimoire that would function as a curse or a blessing).[46]

When reading Nuttall's essay and particularly Huxley, one gets the sense that the visionary state described exceeds the ability of writing to fully capture it. Huxley's reference to the 'miracles, moment by moment of naked existence' offers a certain hyperbole but lacks specific detail as to what constitutes the miraculous aura perceived.[47] Sinclair, by contrast, foregrounds the act of writing in his conceptualisation of the city as a text. It is an integral and productive part of his tactile engagement with London's 'sprawl'. Like his creative colleague Nick Papadimitriou who, in his gazetteer of London's edges *Scarp* (2012), repeatedly declared 'I am Middlesex', Sinclair might seek a disappearance, but this would not involve a step through the doors of perception so much as a rhetorical and corporeal elision with the urban topos.[48]

This difference in approach is made clear in Sinclair's discussion of Ginsberg and Primrose Hill in *The Kodak Mantra Diaries*, his 'documentary' account of *Ah Sunflower!* published in 1971. The text provides a first-hand account of the encounter he recalls in *Blake's London*. In this version the party assembles with only 'vague memories of Blake and bardic ritual', and Ginsberg is discovered trying to read a variant of his poem 'Television was a Baby Crawling Towards that Deathchamber' from *Planet News* (1968).[49] Initially composed in 1961, 'Television' is a coruscating survey of 'brokendown old Blakean America', in which Ginsberg's poetic voice attempts to diagnose the matrix of politics, media and paranoia that seemed in the post-war world to be inaugurating a moment of epochal crisis, a context that was making manifest the 'Death God in the End'.[50] One early refrain in the text is 'I prophesy', a phrase that connotes a revelatory emphasis as if Ginsberg's speaking 'I' – redolent in its cadence of an evangelical preacher – is both imparting a vision and revelling in his divinatory powers, 'one finger raised warning above his gold eye glasses'.[51] In Sinclair's account, by contrast, such spiritual gravitas gives way to a moment of almost comic bathos. The impromptu reading is interrupted first by jeering locals and then by the mysterious appearance of a fire on the hill behind the group. As Sinclair puts it:

> The smoke gets thicker and thicker, a greyblue scarf wraps him from our sight. The whole thing has become apocalyptic. London has gone. The onlookers have gone.

> There are only glimpses of Ginsberg. The red shirt. Black folder spread across his lap. Right hand raised aloft.[52]

London is gone, but only in terms of the skyline as seen from Primrose Hill. What is really obscured here is Ginsberg's attempt at Blakean invocation. In an uncanny echo of the language from 'Television', Sinclair observes how Ginsberg sits with 'prophetic finger raised in the air' before being, quite literally, enveloped by the Big Smoke.[53] The authoritative 'one finger raised warning' of the poem has become a plaintive marker of a poet getting lost. It is as if the urban matter along with all of its possibly hostile energy, the forces that so affected the perambulating Blake, intrudes on and curtails Ginsberg's moment of Romantic fugue, much to Sinclair's fascination.

In offering this reading of *Blake's London* and associated texts by Sinclair, this argument is admittedly doing something of a disservice to the poetry of the *Children of Albion* context. Within the poetry of the 'Underground in Britain' circa 1969, and particularly the examples included in the volume, the binary between Blake the topographer and the Blake of *Glad Day* is not as distinct as Sinclair suggests. Although Nicholas Snowden Willey's 'Les Espaces Interieurs' aligns with Nuttall's conception of 'transcendence' and 'fantasy' in its gravitation towards 'the amazing country of solitude', this is not the consistent mode of the collection.[54] More indicative of a collective tone is Tom McGrath's anti-Vietnam 'The Evidence' with its focus on 'personal realities', as well as Adrian Mitchell's similarly themed poem of outrage 'To Whom It May Concern', with its 'twisted' and burnt human forms.[55] In addition, one also finds the bleak attention to detail in Roy Fisher's 'The Hospital in Winter' with its 'Cold-water-pipes of pain'.[56] These are not poems in which the 'passive, utilitarian barrier of perception' is punctured. Instead, they focus on the often-distressing details either of the urban setting or the wider political situation with the surrounding contemporary context. The ostensible projects are different from that of Sinclair's psychogeographic drift, but the content is similarly material, corporeal and unforgiving in its desire to reveal that which is obscured by general preference.

Much the same could be said of the work of Harry Fainlight, one of the great 'silent' voices among the *Children of Albion* group.[57] Fainlight was a performer at the 'International Poetry Incarnation' at the Albert Hall in 1965, where he gave a now-infamous reading of his hallucinatory epic 'The Spider' (1965). He published one collection in his lifetime, the rare volume *Sussicran* (1965), although several other projects were mooted but went unrealised.[58] Close to Ginsberg, Fainlight was his companion on the Primrose Hill excursion, gaining as a result a walk-on part in the *Kodak Mantra Diaries*. Sinclair describes him as a rather fey character, 'pale with the effort of climbing the hillock … birdlike, uncertain what to make of [the] rubble of cameras'. Here we are told that Fainlight sits with Ginsberg during the visit muttering 'delicate gnomic questions', before asking his fellow poet 'about his dreams'.[59]

One does find early poems like 'To the Autumn Sunbeam God' (1960) reflecting this delicacy. Here, Fainlight assumes a voice that is stereotypically Romantic as his speaker observes, with rhetorical exhortation, smoke from 'burning leaves' and the gentle passage of 'starry-eyed seeds' through the 'timeless corridor' of a sunbeam.[60] Fainlight's treatment of the sun is initially redolent of 'The Ecchoing Green' (1789) with its solar imagery that welcomes 'Spring' with a 'happy' rise. For Blake, though, the image is intentionally seasonal and progressive. It precedes the poem's movement towards the 'darkening Green', a descent of light that signals the eclipse of youthfulness and a passage through life.[61] Fainlight, meanwhile, shies away from such allegory, preferring instead to observe sunlight as a gentle spectacle. The oneiric onanism of 'Sussicran' also valorises an intense solipsism in which the speaker, 'Alone in [their] room' sets up 'the magical apparatus: the / arrangement of mirrors placed to conjure up that other self'.[62] The voice of 'Sussicran' is insulated from anything approximating the external world, with the opening locator of the solitary and possessive 'my room' delimiting the area of articulation and experience.[63] The speaker's only recourse to an additional location comes in the form of two brief similes. The rising energy of the scene is first compared to 'a lightning stripped trunk' while the speaker eventually describes themselves 'Panting [...] as if washed up on a beach'.[64] The primary transaction of the poem is between the speaker and the mirror, the surface on which their 'breath' spreads 'endlessly'.[65] With external scenes thus confined to the poem's metaphorical register, Fainlight offers 'Sussicran' as a closed circuit of a poem, one in which the world it explores is vivid, spectacular, but wholly interiorised.

Elsewhere in his work, Fainlight more typically offers imagery that is not just vividly corporeal but is also suffused with the materiality of the spaces in which his various personae find themselves. In poems like 'Larksong' (1965) – another text Fainlight read at the Albert Hall in 1965 – and particularly 'Six Poems: A Contemporary Sequence', he uses a register of comparable intensity to 'Sussicran' but ultimately plots a very different trajectory. In each, Fainlight surveys the service spaces and edgelands to be found at the city limits: garage forecourts, motorway inclines, chain link fences of industrial enclosure. 'Bypass', the first of his contemporary sequence, takes place on the periphery, in a space of stasis as 'Cars pass' and the dawn rises, the scene 'fixed in the tense of a sub-station generator's / Static, high-tension hum'.[66] Meanwhile, in 'Larksong' he speaks from the 'raw-broken concrete at the airfield's edge'.[67] The poem pits the flight, body and song of a lark, its 'Fistful of blood and feathers', against the 'exhaust blast terrible' of a launching aircraft, here rendered as a 'giant rocket-ship'.[68] For Horovitz, writing in 'Afterwords' – his long survey essay that concludes *Children of Albion* – 'Larksong' is Fainlight's 'apotheosis of lyricism'. Given the extent to which larks appear in the work of Shakespeare, Shelley and not least Blake, Horovitz is right to frame the text as a poem dedicated 'specifically to English poets' and intended to 'rouse up whole galaxies of song'.[69] Blake's painting *Night Startled by the Lark* (1820), an illustration for Milton's 'L'Allegro' (1645) shows the lark as an angel acting as an intermediary between human and divine figures. His note to the image describes how the 'Earth beneath awakes at the Larks voice'.[70]

It is this poetic power that Horovitz refers to in his evaluation. It comes as part of the wider section in the 'Afterwords' essay in which he valorises the ability of poetry to counter the materialistic and technocratic tenor of post-war culture, particularly the overhanging shadow of the nuclear context. He speaks of Gregory Corso's 'Bomb' (1958) and the manner in which the poem, according to Ginsberg, exceeds its subject, becoming 'greater than the bomb'. As Horovitz then puts it, 'modern man must improvise on his inventions if he's not to be enslaved by them'.[71] This point forms the core of his reading of 'Larksong'. As with Fainlight's 'Autumn' there is a delicate appreciation of 'natural' processes, in this case the emission of birdsong and the gesture of flight rather than the sun-flecked movement of seeds. However, 'Larksong' goes on to give such imagery added, comparative force. The song of the title counters the sonic incursion felt elsewhere on the airfield. The lark is described as singing 'ecstatic; unshaken', conscious of but resistant to the 'heart-shaking cathartic roar' of the 'exhaust-blast terrible'.[72] As with Horovitz's poetic birds, Fanlight's 'emblematic' lark refuses to be drowned out by the destructive potential of the machinery lying at the margins of the text. 'Larksong' is thus a reflection on the catalysing power of the lyrical voice.

Fainlight maintained this theme in two parallel texts, 'Trans – "The D.J. Speaks"' (1965) and 'Poem Spoken Through the Loudspeakers, 1965' (1965). The latter's full title, 'Poem spoken through the loudspeakers rigged up at the mouths of the lions in Trafalgar Square – Vietnam Day 1965', provides a clear indication of the context of its composition and the poem's purpose.[73] London's Trafalgar Square was the site of a large-scale anti-Vietnam protest in May 1965 that featured the likes of Joan Baez among the performers, and which stood as a harbinger of the more violent demonstrations in Grosvenor Square in 1968.[74] Fainlight's poem is presented as a statement issued at the rally and, as the title implies, the focus is upon the act of articulation. With reference to the rising 'feedback' between two loudspeakers, Fainlight emphasises the power of the amplified voice.[75] There is little sense of a specific message, and indeed the 'voice' itself appears semi-autonomous. It is not specifically designated as the voice of a speaking 'I', but rather a sound which rises 'from between two lions'.[76] The effect of this 'pure note of terror' is that the lions are galvanised, much like the roused statue(s) that awaken in Sergei Eisenstein's *Battleship Potemkin* (1926).[77] As conduits for this energising voice they become animated; they function not just as vessels but are energised into life. 'The wrath of the lion is the wisdom of God', as Blake put it in *The Marriage of Heaven and Hell* (1790) and when charged with the amplified force Fainlight describes, the lions of his poem similarly assume a semi-divine form becoming entities straight out of the Blakean cosmos: 'Brazen Lion Angels of the Apocalypse'.[78]

In 'Trans', Fainlight approximates a radio voice that addresses 'pill-elves / hi-fi fairy-fury flipsters' in a tone of exhortation, encouraging them out 'onto the rooftops'.[79] With offshore pirate stations such as Radio Caroline broadcasting from

1964 onwards, it is tempting to read 'Trans' as a direct evocation of such rebellious transmissions.[80] As a single statement offered in quotation marks, the poem is framed as a voice received. Whereas 'Poem Spoken Through the Loudspeakers' emphasised the power of vocal amplification, 'Trans' is, correspondingly, a poem of the loudspeaker: a single, resonating address. In an echo of 'The Spider', the voice of 'Trans' is suffused with a supernatural register. The 'wavebands' issuing forth are linked to a 'broomstick' and the sound of each 'group' transmitted with their 'guitars' becomes a 'coven'.[81] Fainlight's broadcast is akin to an act of sorcery, a blast of witch-like power. 'Trans', as an abbreviation of 'transmission' and 'transistor', elides part way through the poem into 'Trance' and 'TranSISters'.[82] 'The Spider', Fainlight's account of a drug experience (inspired, it is suggested, by his use of LSD) refers to a 'cavern full of / wicked sisters' when describing the hallucinatory intensity of the altered state evoked.[83] As with 'Sussicran', the experience is singular and solitary, decidedly introverted. In 'Trans', by contrast, Fainlight recalibrates his language of witchery to convey a process of dissemination, a message that is fed 'round the whole Van Allen belt and back / tingling with ions!'[84] 'Trans', with its focus – in accordance with the implications of the prefix – on that which moves across, beyond or to the other side of a gap or boundary, invests the communicative voice with a distinct sense of transformative potential. Sensitive to the fantastical if not occult implications of tele-technologies – the means by which the voice can be projected beyond the capabilities of the physical body – Fainlight frames his voice as a form of powerful extension, a type of spooky action at a distance.

Paying tribute to Fainlight in the poem 'To be Harry' (1986), Ted Hughes suggested that his writing was fundamentally defined by an act of accuracy, an attempt 'to get it right, just how it felt'.[85] On the page though, this Blakean attention to 'every minute particular' carries a heightening charge. Fainlight's focus is often in the service of the poetic imagination rather than working through a realist concern for fidelity of representation. He is, as in 'Six Poems', concerned with spiritualising the matter of the world, making sacred through a heightened register or through the weight of poetic focus the small details of the landscape before him. In the likes of 'Larksong' and 'Trans', the emphasis is upon the medium of that poetic amplification. On the one hand, Fainlight's voice offers a visionary map of the urban scene, during which he sees the world in a grain of sand. On the other, he is full of the elevating power of *Glad Day*: his poetic persona transcending the material through the transformative potency of his verse.

Writing in his poem 'Memo', Horovitz offered a crystallisation of the dynamics of influence and engagement discussed thus far. Imagining the note coming from 'Wm Blake', Horovitz ventriloquises a chiding voice. His Blake speaks 'to sundry -psychedelinquent whizz kids' who appear 'to assume his name in vain'.[86] The advice is to renounce the point of influence and move on: 'Get wean'd / Or get -stufft'.[87] Horovitz's Blake has little time for the struggling anxiety imagined by Bloom. That his version of Blake is found writing a memo suggests that he is imagined as rather more present and contemporaneously active than the image of a haunting poetic ghost might suggest. He has not been summoned into an act of possession but has sent a mildly irritated memo that carries the tone of someone wishing to be left in peace. That Horovitz would offer this in the clear light of his own, self-consciously Blakean project, suggests that the creative onus in his work is upon progression from a point of inspiration rather than the recitational absorption of such an influence to the point of simulation. Sinclair, Fainlight and the wider mode of visionary poetry reflect this stance in their collective work, even as they stand separately in terms of their themes and execution.

When compared to the likes of Fainlight, Sinclair's position is not reflective of an allegedly 'true' or more accurate reading of Blake and the modern visionary mode. Rather, the difference lies in the trajectory of the projects instigated in the 1960s. For Fainlight and the associated poets discussed, their practice speaks of a certain degree of immediacy, the attempt to see differently and to transform the world around them. The aim, as Nuttall implied, is to take a sidestep, horizontally, 'through' the manifold barriers of 'perception'. Sinclair, by contrast, set out from the 1960s on a project that was resolutely vertical. It was aimed at transmitting the buried layers of London and, going forward, charting its convulsive shifts into capitalised zones. Sinclair thus reads Blake very much as a prophetic poet. In *Blake's London*, he returns to the maps of *Jerusalem* and sites like 'Old Stratford' with a deep sense of the uncanny.[88] By the time he was writing the book, they had become, as written, 'the centre of everything', the enclosed enclaves of Westfield and the Queen Elizabeth Olympic Park.[89] 'Blake anticipates', Sinclair argues, 'future movements, throwing up heretical temples, retail parks, structures that have to be confronted, discussed and debated.'[90] It is this invitation and difficulty that Sinclair encapsulates in his visionary prose and confronts via his topographic sublimity: the covert designs that have shaped and transformed our experience of and access to the city, 'real', imagined and otherwise.

Notes

1 H. Bloom, *The Anxiety of Influence* (Oxford: Oxford University Press, 1973), p. 30.
2 T. S. Eliot, 'The Function of Criticism', in F. Kermode (ed.), *Selected Prose of T. S. Eliot* (London: Faber, 1975), p. 73.
3 Bloom, *The Anxiety of Influence*, p. 29.
4 W. Blake, 'Milton', in D. Erdman (ed.), *The Complete Poetry and Prose of William Blake* (Berkeley: University of California Press, 1988), p. 138.
5 Bloom, *The Anxiety of Influence*, p. 29.
6 H. Bloom, 'Introduction', in H. Bloom (ed.), *William Blake* (New York: Infobase, 2008), p. ix.
7 Bloom, *The Anxiety of Influence*, p. 8.
8 E. Larrissy, *Blake and Modern Literature* (Basingstoke: Palgrave Macmillan, 2006), p. 8.
9 T. Clark and A. Ginsberg, 'Allen Ginsberg', in G. Plimpton (ed.), *Beat Writers at Work: The Paris Review Interviews* (London: Harvill, 1999), p. 55. The interview originally appeared in the *Paris Review*, 37 (1966).
10 *Ibid.*, p. 56.

11 *Ibid.*, p. 57.
12 J. Campbell, *This is the Beat Generation* (London: Vintage, 2000), p. 86.
13 A. Huxley, *The Doors of Perception and Heaven and Hell* (London: Granada, 1977), p. 110.
14 P. B. Shelley, 'A Defence of Poetry', in D. Wu (ed.), *Romanticism: An Anthology* (Chichester: Wiley-Blackwell, 2012), p. 1247; A. Rimbaud, *Complete Works*, trans. P. Schmidt (New York: Harper & Row, 1976), p. 102; C. Olson, 'Projective Verse', in D. Allen and B. Friedlander (eds), *Charles Olson: Complete Prose* (Berkeley: University of California Press, 1997), pp. 239–50. I am grateful to Douglas Field for suggesting these resonances.
15 A. A. Dun, *Vale Royal* (Uppingham: Goldmark, 1995).
16 S. Turner, *Public House* (London: Lux, 2016).
17 The Verve, 'History', *A Northern Soul* (London: Hut, 1995).
18 G. Agamben, 'What Is the Contemporary?', in *What is an Apparatus? and Other Essays*, trans. D. Kishik and Stefan Pedatella (Stanford: Stanford University Press, 2009), p. 42.
19 M. Horovitz, 'Spring Welcomes You to London', in M. Horovitz (ed.), *Children of Albion: Poetry of the Underground in Britain* (Harmondsworth: Penguin, 1969), p. 142.
20 See *Penguin Modern Poets 5: Lawrence Ferlinghetti, Allen Ginsberg, Gregory Corso* (Harmondsworth: Penguin, 1963).
21 Horovitz, 'Spring Welcomes You to London', p. 142.
22 *Ibid.*
23 See Campbell, *This is the Beat Generation*, p. 88. Ginsberg's relationship with the academy, Columbia onwards, was more complex and in some ways more supportive than this binarism suggests. For an indication of this, see M. Schumacher, *Dharma Lion: A Biography of Allen Ginsberg* (Minneapolis: University of Minnesota Press, 2016), p. 23. I am grateful to Luke Walker for reminding me of the importance of this nuance.
24 I. Sinclair, *Blake's London: The Topographic Sublime* (London: The Swedenborg Society, 2012), p. 10.
25 *Ibid.*, p. 12.
26 *Ibid.*
27 *Ibid.*, p. 14.
28 *Ibid.*
29 *Ibid.*
30 *Ibid.*, p. 15.
31 *Ibid.*
32 *Ibid.*, p. 12.
33 P. Ackroyd, *Blake* (London: Reed International, 1995), p. 75.
34 W. Burroughs, *Nova Express* (London: Granada, 1978), p. 60.
35 T. Roszak, 'Youth and the Great Refusal', *The Nation* (25 March 1968), 400.
36 J. Berke, *Counterculture* (London: Fire, 1969), p. 24.
37 Sinclair, *Blake's London*, p. 20.
38 *Ibid.*, p. 20.
39 W. Blake, 'Jerusalem', in Erdman (ed.), *The Complete Poetry and Prose of William Blake*, p. 194.
40 Sinclair, *Blake's London*, p. 20.

41 *Ibid.*, p. 21.
42 I. Sinclair, *Lights Out for the Territory* (London: Granta, 1997), p. 1.
43 J. Nuttall, 'The Menacing Eye', *International Times*, 24 (19 January–1 February 1968), 8–9.
44 W. Blake, 'The Marriage of Heaven and Hell', in Erdman (ed.), *The Complete Poetry and Prose of William Blake*, p. 39.
45 Huxley, *The Doors of Perception*, p. 15.
46 Sinclair, *Lights Out*, p. 1.
47 Huxley, *The Doors of Perception*, p. 15.
48 N. Papadimitriou, *Scarp* (London: Sceptre, 2012), p. 77.
49 I. Sinclair, *The Kodak Mantra Diaries* (Coventry: Beat Scene Press, 2006), p. 44.
50 A. Ginsberg, 'Television was a Baby Crawling Toward that Deathchamber', in *Planet News: 1961–1967* (San Francisco: City Lights Books, 1968), p. 31.
51 *Ibid.*, p. 15.
52 Sinclair, *The Kodak Mantra Diaries*, p. 45.
53 *Ibid.*
54 N. Snowden Willey, 'Les Espaces Interieurs', in Horovitz (ed.), *Children of Albion*, p. 310.
55 T. McGrath, 'The Evidence'; and A. Mitchell, 'To Whom it May Concern', in Horovitz (ed.), *Children of Albion*, p. 199; p. 222.
56 R. Fisher, 'The Hospital in Winter', in Horovitz (ed.), *Children of Albion*, p. 76.
57 See M. Horovitz, 'Afterwords', in Horovitz (ed.), *Children of Albion*, pp. 316–80. Fainlight is mentioned various times, but his writing does not appear in the main body of *Children of Albion*.
58 Harry Fainlight's papers are held at the University of Indiana. The listings for the collection provide details of his unrealised projects. See: Lilly Library, Indiana University, Bloomington, LMC 2604, 'Fainlight MSS, 1935–1982 (bulk 1950–1982)'.
59 Sinclair, *The Kodak Mantra Diaries*, p. 45.
60 H. Fainlight, 'To the Autumn Sunbeam God', in R. Fainlight (ed.), *Harry Fainlight: Selected Poems* (London: Turret Books, 1986), p. 24.
61 W. Blake, 'The Ecchoing Green', in Erdman (ed.), *The Complete Poetry and Prose of William Blake*, p. 8.
62 H. Fainlight, 'Sussicran', in R. Fainlight (ed.), *Harry Fainlight*, p. 47.
63 *Ibid.*
64 *Ibid.*
65 *Ibid.*
66 H. Fainlight, 'Six Poems: A Contemporary Sequence', in R. Fainlight (ed.), *Harry Fainlight*, p. 11.
67 H. Fainlight, 'Larksong', in R. Fainlight (ed.), *Harry Fainlight*, p. 22.
68 *Ibid.*
69 Horovitz, 'Afterwords', p. 370. See also J. V. Baker, 'The Lark in English Poetry', *Prairie Schooner*, 24 (1950), 70–9.
70 For the image and the note in question, see: www.blakearchive.org/copy/but543.1?descId=but543.1.wc.02; www.blakearchive.org/images/bb69.1.2.ms.100.jpg (accessed 26 June 2021).

71 Horovitz, 'Afterwords', p. 370.
72 Fainlight, 'Larksong', p. 22.
73 H. Fainlight, 'Poem Spoken Through the Loudspeakers, 1965', in R. Fainlight (ed.), *Harry Fainlight*, p. 58.
74 For an overview of Trafalgar Square as a site of protest, see **J.** Tranmer, 'London: A Capital of Protest Politics', *Observatoire de la société britannique*, 11 (2011), 177–90.
75 H. Fainlight, 'Poem Spoken Through the Loudspeakers, 1965', p. 58.
76 *Ibid.*
77 *Ibid.* For an overview of *Battleship Potemkin*, see, K. Hariharan, 'Eisenstein and the Potemkin Revolution', *Social Scientist*, 7 (1979), 54–61.
78 Fainlight, 'Poem Spoken Through the Loudspeakers, 1965', p. 58; W. Blake, 'The Marriage of Heaven and Hell', p. 36.
79 H. Fainlight, 'Trans – "The D. J. Speaks"', in R. Fainlight, p. 52.
80 For context on Radio Caroline, see R. C. Humphries, *Radio Caroline: The Pirate Years* (Usk: Oakwood Press, 2003).
81 Fainlight, 'Trans – "The D. J. Speaks"', p. 52.
82 *Ibid.*
83 H. Fainlight, 'The Spider', in P. Whitehead (ed.) *Wholly Communion* (London: Lorrimer, 1965), p. 46.
84 Fainlight, 'Trans – "The D. J. Speaks"', p. 53.
85 T. Hughes, 'To be Harry', in R. Fainlight (ed.), *Harry Fainlight*, p. 5.
86 M. Horovitz, 'Memo', in M. Horovitz (ed.), *Children of Albion*, pp. 147–8 (p. 147). The spacing here is as it appears on the page.
87 *Ibid.*
88 Sinclair, *Blake's London*, p. 52.
89 *Ibid.*
90 *Ibid.*

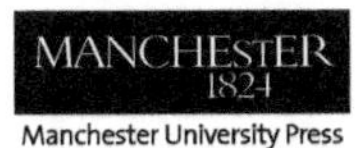

Manchester University Press

'The Place Where Contrarieties are Equally True': Blake and the Science-Fiction Counterculture

JASON WHITTAKER, UNIVERSITY OF LINCOLN

Abstract

This article explores the more detached and ironic view of Blake that emerged in the 1970s compared to appropriations of him in the 1960s, as evident in three science-fiction novels: Ray Nelson's *Blake's Progress* (1977), Angela Carter's *The Passion of New Eve* (1977), and J. G. Ballard's *The Unlimited Dream Company* (1979). In adopting a more antagonistic posture towards Blake, all three of these books reflect increasingly ambivalent attitudes towards the countercultures of the 1960s, and can be read as critical of some of those very energies that the Romantic movement was seen to embody. Thus Nelson rewrites the relationship of William and Catherine, in which the engraver comes under the influence of a diabolic Urizen, while Carter recasts the Prophet Los as a Charles Manson-esque figure. Even Ballard, the most benign of the three, views Blakean energy as a release of potentially dangerous psychopathologies. In all the novels, we see a contrarian use of misprision, rewriting Blake as Blake had rewritten Milton.

Keywords: William Blake; R. F. Nelson; Angela Carter; J. G. Ballard; science fiction; counterculture

In his 1988 book *America*, Jean Baudrillard describes the end of US (and, by implication, western) power, and particularly that period in the 1970s when America did not realise that, to quote the ever-popular phrase of sandwich-board prophets, 'the end is nigh':

> The fifties were the real high spot for the US … and you can still feel nostalgia for those years, for the ecstasy of power, when power held power. In the seventies power was still there, but the spell was broken. That was orgy time (war, sex, Manson, Woodstock). Today the orgy is over. The US, like everyone else, now has to face up to a soft world order, a soft situation. Power has become impotent.[1]

While the soft machine of declining American power was driven by the forces of economic, ecological and social crises, this decline was prophesied – and celebrated – by many of those involved in the counterculture: poets, artists and freethinkers who often invoked William Blake as their own prophet of excess and the end of empire. This article, however, considers the use of Blake at a later stage in the counterculture, beyond the moment of many of the ecstatic hopes of the 1960s and that time when, like so many other aspects of western life, its participants were more concerned with the orgy.

Although it is Allen Ginsberg who is most famous as the spiritual inheritor of Blake, it was perhaps Theodore Roszak – most especially in *The Making of a Counter Culture* (1969) – who invoked Blake as the philosophical precursor of the 1960s. He begins his book with lines from Blake's famous Preface to *Milton a Poem*: 'Rouze up

Bulletin of the John Rylands Library, Volume 98, No. 1 (Spring 2022), pp. 93–106, published by Manchester University Press.
http://dx.doi.org/10.7227/BJRL.98.1.8

O Young Men of the New Age! set your foreheads against the ignorant Hirelings!'[2] Roszak frequently invokes Blake as one of those Dionysian seers such as Friedrich Nietzsche and Jacob Boehme who had most inspired the counterculture, seeing in Ginsberg's poetry of protest not a return to Marx, but rather 'the ecstatic radicalism of Blake'.[3] Tony Tanner, in *City of Words* (1976), observed that the idiosyncratic and individualising forms of American post-war fiction owed much to Los's desire to 'create a system or be enslaved by another man's', and that Blake had defined American writers' process of resistance in *The Marriage of Heaven and Hell.*[4] Sustained critical interest in Blake's 1960s reception began with Robert Bertholf and Annette Levitt's *William Blake and the Moderns* (1982), most notably contributions by Bertholf and Alicia Ostriker on Robert Duncan and Ginsberg, but it has really been in the new millennium that the critics of this New Age have taken stock of the period of the counterculture in relation to the work of the Romantic poet and artist, generally building towards greater nuance than either Roszak's unproblematised appropriation or Ostriker's celebration of the Old Testament prophet and 'primitive' shaman that she found in both Ginsberg and Blake.[5]

Stephen Eisenman provides a useful overview of the reception of Blake into the American counterculture in the 1960s in his essay to the exhibition catalogue, *William Blake and the Age of Aquarius* (2017), drawing attention to how a number of artists including Jim Morrison, Bob Dylan and Jay DeFeo, as well as Beat poets and their contemporaries such as Ginsberg and Duncan, were inspired by Blake. The emphasis, so the now-familiar line of transmission runs, is that they were particularly enthused, as Roszak had been, by Blake's prophetic vision and antinomianism. Peter Otto has traced the influence of Blake and others on the 'latter-day Romantic' Roszak and drawn attention to the recuperation of these countercultural ideals which, in shaping consumer society and postmodern cybercultures, 'have become part of the mainstream culture they were designed to oppose'.[6] Indeed, if there is a key to much contemporary criticism regarding Blake and countercultures, it is that the writers and artists of this period were frequently challenged by – or sought to challenge – Blake. Linda Freedman, for example, in *William Blake and the Myth of America* (2018), while observing that Ginsberg – who viewed Blake as a 'spiritual forefather' – saw the Romantic artist as 'a disillusioned radical, who struggled with the same conflicts as people in modern America', also draws attention to the fact that Ginsberg very deliberately tried to break the hold that he felt Blake had upon him later in his career.[7] Likewise, Luke Walker goes beyond the simplicities of assuming direct lineage between Blake and the Beats, observing that 'Ginsberg's poetic vision of a Blakean Albion is more complex, and more problematic, than might be supposed', not least because the vision of Blake's Albion contained 'nationalist tensions … behind this transgenerational internationalism'.[8]

Some of the criticism of Blake's recuperation by the generation of the counterculture has been more trenchant – for example, James Keery's comments on Michael Horovitz's misunderstanding of Blake's sons and daughters of Albion in the collection *Children of Albion: Poetry of the 'Underground' of Britain* (1969), which provided 'a sentimental image of Blake' very much in contrast with the darker, more savage interpretations of the artist to be found in the poetry of Iain Sinclair.[9]

Indeed, if Horovitz's collection, inspired by the 1965 International Poetry Incarnation which Ginsberg and many other Beats and British underground poets attended, represents the optimistic high-water mark of Blake's influence on counterculture, the three authors to be considered in detail in this article – R. F. Nelson, Angela Carter and J. G. Ballard – are all intensely sceptical of Blake's message. They cannot be said to represent an *anxiety* of influence, for all three are explicit in their indebtedness to Blake, but the prophetic message of antinomian hope that had seemed so self-evident to many in the 1960s seemed much more disturbing in the aftermath of the Manson murders and the oil crisis of 1973. All three writers, in their encounters with Blake, may be seeking to provide their own answers to Baudrillard's question: 'what are you doing after the orgy?'[10]

The first of these three to publish a novel inspired by Blake, Ray Faraday Nelson, was born in New York in 1931 and is best known for his short story 'Eight O'Clock in the Morning' (1963), which was later adapted as the film *They Live* (1988). Having moved to Paris to study, he claimed to have worked with Michael Moorcock and met various members of the Beats such as Ginsberg, Burroughs and Gregory Corso, although it was his friendship with Philip K. Dick that would bear more substantial fruit, including the collaboration *The Ganymede Takeover* (1967). When Jack Newkom introduced Dick to LSD in 1964, it was with Newkom and Nelson that Dick took acid on at least two occasions that year: according to Nelson, on at least one of those instances Dick did not enjoy the experience, but, 'reliving the Roman life of a gladiator', spoke in Latin and experienced a spear thrust through his body.[11] Nelson's use of Blake was the most extensive of the three to be considered here, a science-fiction novel called *Blake's Progress* which was published by Laser Books in 1975. This text, which reads like a pulp fiction crossover between H. G. Wells and Philip K. Dick (but with far worse dialogue), was re-released in an even longer version in 2000 with the title *Timequest*. The earlier novel is a particularly bizarre retelling of Blake's biography mixed in with *The Four Zoas*, elements of Moorcock's works such as *An Alien Heat* (first published 1972), Jerry Cornelius novels such as *The Final Programme* (1968), and the obvious influence of Dick, most notably *The Man in the High Castle* (1962) and *The Three Stigmata of Palmer Eldritch* (1965). In it, the Zoas are (mostly human) time travellers, moving up and down the timestream with Los trying to preserve the order of time, while Urizen seeks to wield power at any cost.

Significantly, throughout the novel it is Catherine (referred to as Kate), Blake's wife, who is the focus of the story: we see William through her eyes, and she is the protagonist. Nelson clearly knows a considerable amount about Blake's life, possibly through Gilchrist or more probably Mona Wilson, whose *The Life of William Blake* was reissued in 1971. His use of such biographical information is erratic and anything but scholarly, and he chooses to interpret his knowledge in a very idiosyncratic fashion; nonetheless, he is very much aware of a wide range of incidents from

Blake's early life. As with all three of the writers considered here, Nelson is particularly concerned with aspects of Blake's sexuality – a very common theme for writers through the 1960s and perhaps indicative of a 'psychoanalytic turn' in fiction from the period. Interestingly, William is portrayed as sexually frigid: his first vision is of Urizen and this is the overriding determiner of his character (which, as we shall see, is the opposite of Ballard's reading). Blake has been overtaken by the Urizenic aspects of his psyche. As he tells Kate:

> I talk to these Zoas. I shake hands with then, touch them. But what are they, Kate? I don't even know that. Are they angels? Sometimes they wear wings, but now I know there's a time in the future when everyone will wear wings and fly. Are they demons? They don't seem really evil, not even Urizen, though the others warn me about him. Urizen's only crime, so far as I can tell, is a passion for knowledge. He must always know the why of everything, and the how. It seems to me he'd be willing to take the universe apart to see how it works.[12]

An early example of this experimentation in the novel is when Urizen kills Kate's mother to see what will happen (he is killed by his own doppelganger as the natural order of things is restored). Before long, William and Catherine start experimenting with visions – a kind of astral travel – where they go to the kingdom of Rintrah and encounter Urizen and Los. Just how bad the novel can be is indicated in one of these early time-travelling visions, in which Urizen, taking Kate and William on a tour of history, has only one item of note to point out – the mini-skirt.[13] Interweaving this sci-fi fantasy with Blake's biography, we learn that the prophetic books are not Blake's, but Urizen's. By the time the pair have moved to Lambeth, it is Kate who is doing all the popular commercial work while William is side-tracked by his visionary (Urizenic) prophetic books.

As the novel progresses, Vala begins to take a prevailing role: with Urizen, she is seeking to control time and it is William's sexual attraction to Vala that explains, in part, Catherine's motivation. This attraction is also the basis for Nelson's psychoanalytic assessment of Blake: William is Urizenically repressed because he desires the harlot, a motivation possibly drawing on the lines from Blake's Notebook: 'In a wife I would desire / What in whores is always found / The lineaments of Gratified desire.'[14] While the pulp nature of *Blake's Progress* is all too evident, at various points Nelson's critical reading of Blake hits upon a significant failing in Blake's work. Susan Fox published 'The Female as Metaphor in William Blake's Poetry' two years after Nelson's novel, but her critique of Blake – that he undermines his own philosophical principle of mutuality by repeated stereotypical depictions of female weakness (a line then taken up by Anne K. Mellor in the early 1980s) – would have struck a chord with *Blake's Progress*.[15]

This interesting critical line is, however, all too easily lost in the plot. One bizarre scene demonstrates what would have happened had Octavian not defeated Anthony and Cleopatra: London would have remained part of a Greek-speaking Roman empire, with Albion at the heart of a global empire. London, now called Golgonooza, is crowned by a gigantic statue of Urizen:

> The statue of naked Urizen stood on the bank of the river, looking down on the vast city of Golgonooza, capital of Albion and capital of the world. No building stood taller than Urizen's head, not even the towers of the temple of Isis. Under Urizen's right foot was a winged serpent, symbol of the sun god, symbol of the red men of Oothoon [America]. The serpent was portrayed as writhing in its death agonies.[16]

William is an unwilling participant in this world: the fact that he is constantly overtaken by his own creations offers a nascent critique of ideas of creativity, and he is treated almost as a child by Vala and Urizen, who have conducted a war of conquest against the indigenous inhabitants of Oothoon (America). When he questions the slavery of this people, Urizen replies: 'What do you want? The world split in half? A world like the one before the Great Change where the United States and Russia stood facing each other with drawn knives for a hundred years?'[17] It is (as ever) Kate who attempts to save him from this world, but the unintended consequences of her actions means that the plague intended for Oothoon destroys Albion instead, echoing the lines from *America a Prophecy*:

> The red fires rag'd! the plagues recoil'd! then rolld they back with fury
> On Albions Angels; then the Pestilence began in streaks of red
> Across the limbs of Albions Guardian, the spotted plague smote Bristols
> And the Leprosy Londons Spirit, sickening all their bands.[18]

Order is only restored – following the bizarre logic of the novel – when the pair travel back in time to ensure that Anthony and Cleopatra lose the battle of Actium.

They are later caught up in a more terrible alternate world which has been taken over by lizard men, ruled by Urizen who changed things before the dawn of history. In this version, Blake's brother, Robert, turns out to be a time traveller too, who sees in the future that Urizen and Vala will themselves become mindless serpents. How Kate and William defeat this is by going back to the time of the deluge (not a myth after all) and discovering that Urizen had robots hunt down and destroy all humans so that lizards would evolve as the supreme life force. William and Kate insinuate themselves into a lizard tribe and Kate gives birth to Orc, a lizard baby; it appears all of them will change into lizards too until Kate wills them to return to the 'ordinary' universe of 1794. This utterly bizarre development appears only tangentially connected to Blake's work until we call to mind the following lines from *The Book of Urizen*, outlining the conception and birth of Orc to Enitharmon:

> A time passed over, the Eternals
> Began to erect the tent;
> When Enitharmon sick,
> Felt a Worm within her womb.
>
> Yet helpless it lay like a
> Worm In the trembling womb
> To be moulded into existence
>
> All day the worm lay on her bosom
> All night within her womb

The worm lay till it grew to a serpent
With dolorous hissings & poisons
Round Enitharmons loins folding,

Coild within Enitharmons womb
The serpent grew casting its scales,
With sharp pangs the hissings began
To change to a grating cry,
Many sorrows and dismal throes,
Many forms of fish, bird & beast,
Brought forth an Infant form
Where was a worm before.[19]

This is one of several examples in Nelson's novel where an apparently inexplicable event, and one that is bizarre in terms of the development of the plot, can be seen clearly to have its source in Blake's works.

Blake's Progress ends with William and Kate together in 1827 on the day of William's death when he tells her:

> I've never been a real artist, never been able to give life to the things in my mind. It's when we work together … My rough clumsy sketches and your fantastic finished work. It's when we've worked together that we've made pictures that could have come from the hand of Rafael or DaVinci. All the prophetic books, all the books based on the things we did in distant times and places. We did them together, Kate![20]

Nelson thus does two fundamental rewrites: of Blake's life – particularly his relations to Catherine – and of the history of his world in the 1790s. There are some interesting mistakes in the biography, such as the reference to Thomas Butts as Blake's patron in 1794 (Butts only befriended the Blakes after the failure of *Night Thoughts* in 1797), but this error probably stems from Mona Wilson introducing Butts in the chapter on Lambeth. The whole is a rather absurd exploration of notions of creativity – not so much an unconscious misprision of Blake as the launch pad for a deliberate swerving away into science fiction that allows Nelson to postulate critical observations regarding the psychosexual sources for Blake's own creativity.

If Nelson offers a strange, even oblique, reading of the psychosexual sources of Blake's creativity in *Blake's Progress*, then the anti-feminist aspects of Blake's philosophy – outlined by Fox and Mellor at the end of the 1970s and early 1980s – were very clearly a driving force for the second novel to be considered here: Angela Carter's *The Passion of New Eve*. Published by Victor Gollancz in 1977, the novel is set in a near-future dystopian United States where civil war has broken out, and the connections to Blake's work – particularly *Milton a Poem* – have been noted by a number of scholars. Published after *The Infernal Desire Machines of Doctor Hoffman* (1972), it continues many of the sado-masochistic themes of that novel (and Carter herself may have been influenced by the conflation of Blake and de Sade in Bataille's *Literature and Evil*, first translated in 1973). Christopher Ranger has described Blake and Carter as 'friendly enemies', and her own attitude to him is best summed up by a comment in her introduction to the *Virago Book of Fairy Tales*:[21]

> When I was a girl, I thought that everything Blake said was holy, but now I am older and have seen more of life, I treat his aphorisms with the affectionate scepticism appropriate to the exhortations of a man who claimed to have seen a fairy's funeral.[22]

The Passion of New Eve may owe as much to Blake's *America a Prophecy* as to *Milton a Poem*, beginning as it does with Locke's epigram – 'in the beginning all the world was America' – but while she may treat Blake with scepticism, she was inspired in her critical stance towards Enlightenment thinking by him and de Sade. At the beginning of the novel, Evelyn is told 'the age of reason is over' by a Czech soldier guarding the university where he is to work; New York had been built as a city of reason, so its fall will be much worse.[23]

Leilah is the dark shadow (most probably a reference to Blake's 'Shadowy Female') of America and, as we discover by the end of the novel, becomes Lilith to Eve. While she is increasingly sceptical of Blake, like Ballard, Carter takes from the earlier artist (and, indeed, from fairy tales) the tendency to write in archetypes. As we shall again see with Ballard, she is also concerned with the return of repressed desire, invoking images of 'Rahab the Harlot' in her discussions of Evelyn's relations with Leilah and referencing the proverb of Hell, 'you never know what is enough unless you know what is more than enough' when Evelyn says of his lover: 'I had enough of her, then more than enough.'[24]

Leaving Leilah (after making her undergo an abortion that goes horribly wrong and leaves her incapable of bearing other children), Evelyn travels West into the desert, where he is taken to Beulah – the 'place where contrarieties are equally true' – and which is described as follows:

> Beulah is a profane place. It is a crucible. It is the home of the woman who calls herself the Great Parricide, also glories in the title of the Great Emasculator; ecstasy their only anaesthetic, the priest of Cybele sheared off their parts to exalt her, ran bleeding, psalmodising, through the streets. This woman has many names, but her daughters call her Mother.[25]

Beulah is where the connection to *Milton a Poem* is made most explicit, as in the following lines from the beginning of Book II:

> There is a place where Contrarieties are equally True
> This place is called Beulah, It is a pleasant lovely Shadow
> Where no dispute can come. Because of those who Sleep.
> Into this place the Sons & Daughters of Ololon descended
> With solemn mourning into Beulahs moony shades & hills
> Weeping for Milton: mute wonder held the Daughters of Beulah
> Enrapturd with affection sweet and mild benevolence

Beulah is evermore Created around Eternity; appearing
To the Inhabitants of Eden, around them on all sides.
But Beulah to its Inhabitants appears within each district
As the beloved infant in his mothers bosom round incircled
With arms of love & pity & sweet compassion. But to
The Sons of Eden the moony habitations of Beulah,
Are from Great Eternity a mild & pleasant Rest.[26]

As with Susan Fox's critique of Blake, it is the inferior stereotype of Beulah compared to Eden which most drives Carter's anger. As a direct refutation of the earlier Romantic, she makes Beulah a place of struggle and conflict – not rest – and while it draws on mythic elements such as the cult of Cybele, it is also presented in scientific and technological terms; almost Urizenic as a site of experimentation and operation where Evelyn will be medically transformed into Eve. Carter also plays with other fundamentalist stereotypes employed by Blake, such as his categorisation of Los as Time and Enitharmon as space when she writes: 'Time is a man, space is a woman.'[27] Eve becomes a woman who does not understand the space of America where she is repeatedly lost, a man who runs out of time repeatedly.

Escaping Mother, Eve is captured and enslaved by Zero the Poet (or Carter's caricature of Los the Prophet) who 'adored the desert because he hated humanity' and once wrote his poetry down but found it disgusted him.[28] This misogynistic, Charles Manson-esque figure may be a wry commentary on the adaptation of Blake by the counterculture and Beats – an end result of the indulgence of masculinity that is criticised in an incredibly brutal fashion. Zero's rape of Eve is grotesque but also desultory, over in a sentence (and in this respect is surprisingly close to the description of Oothoon's rape by Bromion in *Visions of the Daughters of Albion*). The seven women who live with him – and it is clear, they are there in the end because they choose to be, he having no power – along with Eve find themselves in a deserted town ironically described as the 'New Jerusalem'.[29] Zero assumes that he is in control of the cult he has generated but it becomes clear that without the *willing* actions of his female followers he has no power at all. Zero has a bust of Nietzsche on his desk, who notoriously reminded his readers to take a whip when they went to women, and this pseudo-intellectualism is a general comment by Carter on the Romantics as a whole (he is, after all as much a Byronic as Blakean parody, a comparison that is made explicit a few pages later). Zero is a contrary to Mother that Eve seems to believe will be synthesised in the character that Zero is hunting down, the faded, femme-fatale film star, Tristessa, who herself turns out only to be masquerading as a cisgender woman.

The terms used to describe Tristessa when Zero finds her ('Platonic shadow show, an illusion that could fill my own emptiness with marvellous, imaginary things as long as … the movie lasted') suggests a negation rather than emanation – although for Carter, both terms probably amount to the same thing.[30] Following the revelation of Tristessa's male-sexed body, the character is portrayed as enacting a stereotype of the feminine form, in which the ideal woman is no more than a projection of male desire. The parody wedding that ends the bacchanalia in Tristessa's mansion is thus a never-ending series of shifting identities in which 'I only mimicked what I had been; I did not become it' (an interesting rebuff to 'they became what they beheld', a line often repeated throughout *Jerusalem the Emanation of the Giant Albion*).[31] Theirs is a 'double wedding' with both the groom, both the bride.

The entire novel, then, forms a critique of Blake's limited notions of sexual identity (Zoas, emanations, spectres). Blake is one of the most interesting figures of the eighteenth century to open up ideas of what sexual identity is, but ultimately remains bound to male/female duality. The novel ends in civil war in California – the end of the world both in space and in time: its apocalypse. Here Eve meets Leilah again (and discovers she is the daughter of Mother and her true name is Lilith). Leilah's antithesis is not Eve, but Sophia, the Divine Virgin to her Harlot. This in turn offers an interesting insight into the limitations of archetypes as used by Carter as much as Blake – that such archetypes too easily become stereotypes. Those archetypes are invoked here in a Jungian sense in the final scenes, where Eve descends through caves to Mother in lines which often echo *The Marriage of Heaven and Hell* or *The Book of Urizen*. Eve is reborn a woman in Eden – and *not* in secondary Beulah.

The final in the triptych of sci-fi novels considered here, J. G. Ballard's *The Unlimited Dream Company* (1979), is a non-Christian retelling of Blake's *Milton a Poem*, an attempt to rewrite Blake using Freud, Jung and surrealism. The central character – simply named Blake – is, we learn, experiencing the final moments of a dying fantasy as he drowns in the Cessna airplane he has stolen and crash-landed in the Thames near to the suburb of Shepperton, where Ballard lived most of his life after returning to London following the Second World War. For much of the novel, Blake is more like Luvah or Orc than Los: a hypersexualised and violent rapist who portrays the spirit of Orc in the worst possible way, drawing on the hints of that avatar of rebellion as depicted in the Preludium to *America a Prophecy*. In the pre-Shepperton world, Blake is derelict and dangerous: his powers, however, are restricted. In the life-in-death he experiences in Shepperton, those powers become almost unlimited, bound only by the strange horizon of Shepperton itself.

Throughout the novel there are many parallels to Max Ernst and other surrealists as well as Blake, a feature of Ballard's writing since at least his 1962 novel, *The Drowned World*. Thus Blake's assumption of a bird-like body is akin to Ernst's bird avatar, Loplop, while the description of Shepperton as an Amazonian town is like the grattage cities of the forest scraped by Ernst in the 1920s. Likewise, the depiction of Miriam in her wedding dress draws upon the painting *The Robing of the Bride* (1940), especially in chapter 31 where she is dressed for a particularly appalling ritual in which, after a dismal orgy among the people of Shepperton, she is raped to death by Blake. As such the novel deals with a particular state of psychosis: when we are introduced to him, he is a failure in everything (mercenary pilot, Jesuit priest, writer of pornography) who, after the attempted murder of his fiancée, steals a Cessna and crash lands near Shepperton studios.[32] This becomes the Felpham of the novel, England's green and pleasant land transferred to the suburbs, but rather than William Blake struggling to recuperate a Urizenic Milton who had excluded sexuality from his vision of heaven, Ballard is competing with a demonic, Orc-like Blake who – in his invocations to travel to the palace of wisdom via the road of excess – opens the door to the most damaging psychoses of post-1960s liberation.

As he crashes, he has an apocalyptic vision of the end of the world (what we will realise is his own end) but instead returns to life, surrounded by characters (Miriam, Wingate, Mrs St Cloud, Stark) who – as in Carter's and Nelson's novels – operate as types from his unconscious rather than rounded characters. Slowly, he discovers that he is trapped in Shepperton and, as a truly dangerous and priapic rapist, seeks the engine by which to flee the town:

> but I needed to go further, to undermine the trust between wives and husbands, between fathers and sons. I wanted them to cross the lines that divided children and parents, species and biological kingdoms, the animate and inanimate. I wanted to destroy the restraints that separated mother and son, father and daughter.[33]

His response to rapes and attempted murder are chilling: 'these crimes and lusts were the first stirrings of the benign forces revealed to me in Shepperton'.[34] There is a kind of wonder to Blake's projections within the suburb: in his dreams of being a bird, the other occupants become birds which he gradually absorbs into his body, and the town is transformed by lurid, tropical vegetation. In this milieu, he becomes as a god and, in the chapter 'The Life Engine', the inhabitants of Shepperton – now naked – build shrines to Blake as a pagan deity. In this respect, perhaps, he is like Satan or, as Alistair Cormack observes in his discussion of the novel, even Urizen, a counterfeit god.[35] The nakedness of the town's citizens implies that they have returned to Eden, but this Eden is itself false, the implication of its falsehood being given strength by the fact that only Blake can see that all these people are naked – in other words, it is another psychotic projection on his part.

This theme of divinity is repeated throughout the later part of the novel, as in the chapter 'The Motorcade', where he describes himself as 'a god reborn from the dead' and 'the first living creature to escape death, to rise above mortality to become a god'.[36] Blake sees himself as 'a single chimeric god uniting all life within me'.[37] In terms that William Blake would have recognised, the Blake of *The Unlimited Dream Company* has become Satan – one god, one priest, one king – because he wants to consume everything to escape Shepperton (transformed in the novel into a surrealist hell) and preserve his own life. It is, however, Miriam's death that begins his return to life: he has sacrificed Ololon. Blake's answer to every difficulty has been to consume more via rape, murder, even a kind of cannibalistic absorption. His conception of his own body, transferring the spaces of Shepperton to his body as Blake describes London and Britain mapped onto Albion, is extremely Blakean, though in this case it is 'the small suburbs of my body'. One passage, however, demonstrates just how far the indebtedness to William Blake goes:

> The townspeople of Shepperton were hiding in their bedrooms, but at dusk a party of women approached the memorial and began to abuse me. They were mothers of the children I had taken into me, those girls and boys whose distant souls ran through the dark galleries deep within me and alone kept me alive.[38]

This description as a dark pastoral is reminiscent of the dark pastorals of *Songs of Innocence*, but also of that moment in *Milton* when Los stands within Satan:

> I also stood in Satans bosom & beheld its desolations!
> A ruind Man: a ruind building of God not made with hands;
> Its plains of burning sand, its mountains of marble terrible:
> Its pits & declivities flowing with molten ore & fountains
> Of pitch & nitre: its ruind palaces & cities & mighty works;
> Its furnaces of affliction in which his Angels & Emanations
> Labour with blackend visages among its stupendous ruins
> Arches & pyramids & porches colonades & domes:
> In which dwells Mystery Babylon, here is her secret place
> From hence she comes forth on the Churches in delight
> Here is her Cup filld with its poisons, in these horrid vales
> And here her scarlet Veil woven in pestilence & war:
> Here is Jerusalem bound in chains, in the Dens of Babylon[39]

The Blake of *The Unlimited Dream Company* is clearly identified here as Satan: after the death of Miriam, there is no mistaking that Shepperton has now become hell: instead of the beautiful ambiguity of Ernst's jungle forest and the flight of glorious if threatening birds, other characters such as Stark try to use Blake to escape the suburbs, turning to a slaughter of every animal they can find when that is unsuccessful. In such circumstances, flies transfer from Blake's body onto the corpses, transforming him into Beelzebub (and doubtless an allusion to Golding). Soon afterwards, even the last of the birds are killed and Blake describes Shepperton as 'a garden of cancers'.[40]

It is at this moment that the animals in Stark's zoo give up their life for Blake, an act of self-sacrifice that shows him what he must do. Born again, 'the father of myself', he gives himself away, dismembering himself to cure everyone in Shepperton (and thus becoming Christ-like).[41] This leads to a final act of revelation, a day of judgement in chapter 39 ('Departure') where the inhabitants of Shepperton fly away, leaving Blake behind and allowing him to raise Miriam (his Ololon) having confronted his own Satan, the skeleton in the cockpit. That final confrontation, where Blake struggles with the skeleton that he finally recognises to be himself, his drowned body that he has sought to escape, is the same revelation that Milton experiences in *Milton a Poem*:

> Satan! my Spectre! I know my power thee to annihilate
> And be a greater in thy place, & be thy Tabernacle
> A covering for thee to do thy will, till one greater comes
> And smites me as I smote thee & becomes my covering.
> Such are the Laws of thy false Heavns! but Laws of Eternity

Are not such: know thou: I come to Self Annihilation
Such are the Laws of Eternity that each shall mutually
Annihilate himself for others good, as I for thee
Thy purpose & the purpose of thy Priests & of thy Churches
Is to impress on men the fear of death; to teach
Trembling & fear, terror, constriction; abject selfishness
Mine is to teach Men to despise death & to go on
In fearless majesty annihilating Self, laughing to scorn
Thy Laws & terrors, shaking down thy Synagogues as webs
I come to discover before Heavn & Hell the Self righteousness
In all its Hypocritic turpitude, opening to every eye
These wonders of Satans holiness shewing to the Earth
The Idol Virtues of the Natural Heart, & Satans Seat
Explore in all its Selfish Natural Virtue & put off
In Self annihilation all that is not of God alone:
To put off Self & all I have ever & ever Amen[42]

As Blake rewrote Milton as a Urizenic Satan, so Ballard rewrites Blake in *The Unlimited Dream Company* as an Orcish devil, retelling Christian stories for a post-Christian generation that owes more to Freud and Nietzsche but has not yet reconciled itself to the pagan mythopoetic narratives that still drive its unconscious. The ultimate question of the novel is: what is the role of love in a world without God? Blake is driven by his selfishness throughout the novel and, like Milton in Blake's original poem, he must give up that selfhood.

The most immediate and compelling facet of these three novels is that, in a very short space of time, three authors provided highly engaged and direct reformulations of the work of William Blake, with at least two of them (Nelson and Ballard) paraphrasing significant parts of Blake's poetry to provide the plot and direction for their own works. Blake had, of course, been gaining ground as an influence on modern art and literature throughout the twentieth century, and with the impetus of the Beats, Ginsberg in particular, he had assumed a central role as prophet of the counterculture. And yet all three writers assume a very different role for this prophet in their fiction: if Ginsberg and several of his contemporaries had seen the Romantic and poet as the precursor to their own struggles against post-war technocratic society, Nelson, Carter and Ballard are all united in a much more sceptical vision of the value of Blake's poetry. The author of *The Marriage of Heaven and Hell* who had proclaimed 'Energy is Eternal Delight' became for them a troubling progenitor of the excesses of the preceding decade.[43] All three engage in deliberate misprision of Blake, and the fact that their distortions of the original inspiration *are* deliberate indicate that their work is clearly not an unconscious anxiety of influence. The sexual liberation of the 1960s was anything but complete, and all three are – in the context of the general reception of the Romantic in the 1970s – surprisingly attuned to the accusations of misogyny that were beginning to filter through Blake studies. If the earlier phase of the counterculture had looked upon his works with the cloudless vision of innocence, then in Nelson, Carter and Ballard we see what happens when the eyes of experience must consider what shape society will take once the orgy is finished.

Notes

1 J. Baudrillard, *America* (London: Verso, 1988), p. 117.
2 D. Erdman (ed.), *The Complete Poetry and Prose of William Blake* (Berkeley: University of California Press, 1988), p. 95.
3 T. Roszak, *The Making of a Counter Culture: Reflections on the Technocratic Society and Its Youthful Opposition* (Berkeley: University of California Press, 1995 [1968]), p. 126.
4 T. Tanner, *City of Words: American Fiction, 1950–1970* (London: Jonathan Cape, 1971), p. 109.
5 A. Ostriker, 'Blake, Ginsberg, Madness, and the Prophet as Shaman', in R. J. Bertholf and A. S. Levitt (eds), *William Blake and the Moderns* (Albany: State University of New York Press, 1982), p. 127.
6 P. Otto, '"Rouze up O Young Men of the New Age!": William Blake, Theodore Roszak, and the Counter Culture of the 1960s–1970s', in S. Clark, T. Connolly and J. Whittaker (eds), *Blake 2.0: William Blake in Twentieth-Century Art, Music and Culture* (Houndmills: Palgrave, 2012), p. 29.
7 L. Freedman, *William Blake and the Myth of America: From the Abolitionists to the Counterculture* (Oxford: Oxford University Press, 2018), pp. 89, 116.
8 L. Walker, 'Allen Ginsberg's Blakean Albion', *Comparative American Studies An International Journal*, 11 (2013), 227–8.
9 J. Keery, 'Children of Albion: Blake and Contemporary British Poetry', in S. Clark and J. Whittaker (eds), *Blake, Modernity and Popular Culture* (Houndmills: Palgrave, 2007), p. 100.
10 J. Baudrillard, *America*, p. 30.
11 L. Sutin, *Divine Invasions: A Life of Philip K. Dick* (New York: Carroll & Graf, 2005), p. 141.
12 R. F. Nelson, *Blake's Progress* (Toronto: Laser Books, 1975), p. 32.
13 *Ibid.*, p. 47.
14 Erdman, *The Complete Poetry and Prose of William Blake*, p. 474.
15 S. Fox, 'The Female as Metaphor in William Blake's Poetry', *Critical Inquiry*, 3 (1977), 507–19; A. K. Mellor, 'Blake's Portrayal of Women', *Blake: An Illustrated Quarterly*, 16 (1982/3), 148–54.
16 Nelson, *Blake's Progress*, p. 79.
17 *Ibid.*, p. 81.
18 Erdman, *The Complete Poetry and Prose of William Blake*, pp. 56–7.
19 *Ibid.*, p. 79.
20 Nelson, *Blake's Progress*, p. 173.
21 C. Ranger, 'Friendly Enemies: A Dialogical Encounter between William Blake and Angela Carter', in Clark and Whittaker (eds), *Blake, Modernity and Popular Culture*, pp. 140–50.
22 A. Carter, *The Virago Book of Fairy Tales* (London: Virago, 1991), p. x.

23 A. Carter, *The Passion of New Eve* (London and New York: Victor Gollancz, 1977), p. 13.
24 Erdman, *The Complete Poetry and Prose of William Blake*, p. 37; Carter, *The Passion of New Eve*, p. 31.
25 Carter, *The Passion of New Eve*, p. 46.
26 Erdman, *The Complete Poetry and Prose of William Blake*, p. 129.
27 Carter, *The Passion of New Eve*, p. 50.
28 *Ibid.*, p. 85.
29 *Ibid.*, p. 100.
30 *Ibid.*, p. 110.
31 *Ibid.*, p. 132.
32 J. G. Ballard, *The Unlimited Dream Company* (New York: Holt, Rinehart and Winston, 1979), p. 7.
33 *Ibid.*, p. 171.
34 *Ibid.*, p. 171.
35 A. Cormack, 'J.G. Ballard and William Blake: Historicizing the Reprobate Imagination', in J. Baxter and R. Wymer (eds), *J.G. Ballard: Visions and Revisions* (Houndmills: Palgrave, 2012), pp. 142–59.
36 Ballard, *The Unlimited Dream Company*, pp. 185, 186.
37 *Ibid.*, p. 191.
38 *Ibid.*, p. 197.
39 Erdman, *The Complete Poetry and Prose of William Blake*, p. 139.
40 Ballard, *The Unlimited Dream Company*, p. 208.
41 *Ibid.*, p. 213.
42 Erdman, *The Complete Poetry and Prose of William Blake*, p. 139.
43 *Ibid.*, p. 34.

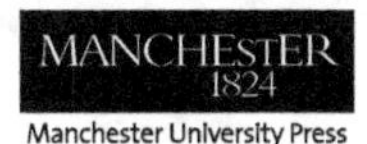

Manchester University Press

A Cosmopolitan Case Study: Countercultural Blake in the Therapoetic Practice of maelstrÖm reEvolution

FRANCA BELLARSI, UNIVERSITÉ LIBRE DE BRUXELLES

Abstract

This article explores the reception and transformation of William Blake's countercultural legacy by focusing on the neo-Romantic resurgences within maelstrÖm reEvolution, an experimental performance and arts collective based in Brussels but with heavy transnational affiliations. In relation to the company's neo-shamanic and therapeutic conception of *poiesis*, Blake is an inspirational figure amongst a broader family of mentors ranging from Beat Generation writers to Arthur Rimbaud and Alexandro Jodorowsky. The Blake–maelstrÖm connection is here examined for the first time. Blending classical reception studies with a broader interest in the intersections between *poiesis* and the 'sacred', this article approaches countercultural Blake as the archetypal embodiment of the shamanic poet. More specifically, it reflects on how, as the poet of 'double-edged madness' and 'Spiritual Strife', Blake's subversion of alienation into ecstasy feeds maelstrÖm's own 'therapoetic' experimentalism and psycho-aesthetic endeavours to restore the lines of communication between the 'visible' and the 'invisible'.

Keywords: maelstrÖm reEvolution; Blake reception; Beat Generation; neo-shamanism; ecstasy; performance art; therapoetry

This article explores an instance of the reception and transformation of William Blake's countercultural legacy by focusing on the neo-Romantic resurgences embodied by maelstrÖm reEvolution, an experimental performance collective based in Brussels but with marked transnational affiliations. Though heavily indebted to the Beat Generation, the company's neo-shamanic and therapeutic conception of poetry and art is driven by a number of other major literary, philosophical and esoteric influences, Blake included. This array of sources particularly inspires maelstrÖm's striving for the transmuting of energy in performance and the related search for a contemporary form of personal secular mysticism.

When it comes to either direct or indirect routes of transmission, the Blake–maelstrÖm dialogue has never been examined before. Starting with the indirect paths of Blake's reception within maelstrÖm, I first look at the sustained inspiration the group draws from the production of the Beat Generation, and then turn to its deep connections to other, more heterogeneous sources which, together with Blake, cohere into a kind of 'esoteric family' of visionary dissent. As regards the direct roads of encounter with Blake's work, I here present some of the information gathered in a personal, one-day interview with David Giannoni, the founder of maelstrÖm, as well as in written exchange with Tom Buron and Tom Nisse, two other central poetic voices in the collective who agreed to share their individual perception of Blake in answering a detailed questionnaire.[1] Thus, this enquiry into the connections between Blake and the maelstrÖm reEvolution company blends classical reception studies with a broader interest in the intersections between *poiesis* and the 'sacred'. As such, this article forms part of a larger attempt to understand how the religious notion of 'ecstasy' transposes to literature and art.[2]

My exploration of the links between Blake and maelstrÖm begins with a reflection on Blake's neo-shamanic conception of the poet, and on how the 'path of unknowing' inherent in it ties in with countercultural aspirations of deconditioning in general. After a brief recapitulation of the history of the performance group, I discuss the various paths of transmission linking maelstrÖm's neo-Romantic dynamics to Blake's countercultural legacy. My outline of Blake's reception within maelstrÖm is also interlaced with considerations on how the company's dialogue with the English visionary seeps into the healing journeys of initiation they attempt to create in performance and print, so as to provoke a psycho-aesthetic overcoming of perception rooted in dualism.

Which Version of Blake? The Poet as Shaman

When it comes to the reception of Blake, the initial question always has to be 'which version of the English poet-artist is being predominantly embraced here?' In the case of maelstrÖm reEvolution, as suggested by the notions of morphing and evolving embedded in the very name of the performance group, it is Blake, the author of a mythopoetic verse of psycho-spiritual journeying and change, who should preoccupy us first and foremost – even if that facet cannot entirely be dissociated from his more politically and socially dissenting ones. In other words, it is the *poet as shaman* who provides the best point of entry into the territory where Blake's and maelstrÖm's respective universes meet.

In pre-modern cultures, the shaman is not only a go-between linking the material and immaterial worlds because he or she can access states of altered consciousness. He or she is also a healer, using vision, trance and a wilful derangement of normal empirical perception to enable and facilitate psychological re-integration for individuals and the community.[3] Moreover, as a lifelong calling, shamanism involves suffering and sacrifice, the shaman often operating as a 'wounded healer' who helps others retrieve their 'lost soul'.[4]

Though the transfer of the term 'shamanic' from anthropology to art may seem like a debatable, facile New Age appropriation in some cases, one cannot accuse Blake of fake ecstatic mysticism. Not only did he experience literal visions in his lifetime, but his engagement with verbal and visual texts was also spiritual and always meant to remedy the limitations of the empirical senses, which, for him, wrongly and artificially severed the material from the spiritual, the visible from the invisible:[5]

> But first the notion that man has a body distinct from his soul, is to be expunged; this I shall do, by printing in the infernal method, by corrosives, which in Hell are salutary and medicinal, melting apparent surfaces away, and displaying the infinite which was hid.

> If the doors of perception were cleansed every thing would appear to man as it is: infinite.

> For man has closed himself up, till he sees all things thro' narrow chinks of his cavern.[6]

Blake's poetic and artistic practice bears deep analogies with the trance-like journeying of the traditional shaman, particularly when it comes to skilfully making poison and disease a part of the remedy leading towards healing.[7] As Alicia Ostriker explains, Blake and Los, his poetic alter ego, take wilful and repeated plunges into a fallen, insane world so as to give 'a body to Falshood that it may be cast off for ever',[8] since delving deeper into the evil generated by false consciousness turns out, paradoxically, to be the necessary precondition for a redemption of both perceiver and perceived.[9] Put differently, Blake manages to transform ordinary madness – or the endured insanity that a hyper-rationalist and utilitarian society imposes upon the individual – into ecstatic madness, a spatial-temporal derangement of the senses that liberates the mind from the limiting power of narrow, Reason-based perception only.[10] In Blake's own words:

> Cowper came to me & said. O that I were insane always I will never rest. Can you not make me truly insane. I will never rest till I am so. O that in the bosom of God I was hid. You retain health & yet are as mad as any of us all – over us all – mad as a refuge from unbelief – from Bacon Newton & Locke.[11]

For both Blake and the pre-modern shaman, the subversion of madness as a *disease* symptomatic of an 'alienation of the soul'[12] into crazy ecstasy as an expression of *release* from affliction supposes shamans taking upon themselves the ills of others, so as to skilfully cure blocked energies and restore the manifold circulations in a world at heart interconnected at all levels.[13] In the shamanic world, the *spiritual* is thus fundamentally enmeshed with the *therapeutic*, and vice versa, just as the *spiritual* and the *physical* are also tightly intertwined.[14] Healing may be linked to mental travel from visible universes to connected invisible ones, but it cannot possibly be done outside *embodied ritual*, 'the spirit world, the human world, and the nature world' being 'wholly one in essence, though different in appearance'.[15]

The journeying through overlapping material and immaterial universes in correspondence with one another, the transformation of insanity into ecstasy through the wilful distortion of time and space, as well as the very physical nature of the visionary, trance-inducing process, are all elements that, by analogy, resonate with Blake's literary and engraving work, as well as with his pursuit of perceptual cleansing through a dialectal interplay of opposites undoing the conventional binaries of dualism. Closer to us in time, by analogy too, these are likewise multiple echoes of the therapeutic or, better said, 'therapoetic' approach to writing and performance that a creative group like maelstrÖm cultivates by way of challenging an exclusively hyper-rational and hyper-technological engagement with the 'real'.[16] As for Blake and his archetype of the shamanic poet, Los, subverting madness as disease into ecstasy as release and re-humanisation lies at the heart at maelstrÖm's 'therapy of illiteracy',[17] a psycho-aesthetic deconditioning which refuses to see body and mind, the visible and the invisible, and the holy and the profane as irreconcilable opposites.

maelstrÖm as a Neo-Shamanic Concept

In Brussels today, maelstrÖm is a polymorphic arts collective merging an independent bookstore and publishing house with a series of workshops, readings and live performances all year round. Each spring, the latter culminate in its 'fiEstival', the poetry festival-*cum*-street party through which the collective connects not only with a number of internationally like-minded poets and artists, but also with the multi-ethnic and socially diverse reality of the city. As detailed in *The Routledge Handbook of International Beat Literature*, maelstrÖm reEvolution constitutes a kind of Brussels reincarnation of the original City Lights in San Francisco and was historically the brainchild of Italian poet David Giannoni, who, after a youth spent in France and the USA, made Brussels his home in maturity. In its formative phase, Giannoni's project also bore the influence of vital mentors like the Italian poet and publisher Antonio Bertoli (1957–2015), the American Beat poet and publisher Lawrence Ferlinghetti (1919–2021), and the Chilean film-maker and Tarot specialist Alexandro Jodorowsky (b. 1929).[18] It is this vital synergy that helped galvanise the *maelstrÖm* magazine founded in 1990 into the hybrid experimental performance and publishing venture which the arts collective represents today. It is also through such associations that the group absorbed some of the neo-Romantic and Gnostic energies of the Beat Generation, alongside the provocative outlook and performance formats of other avant-garde influences like the Dadaists or Situationists.[19]

However, it bears recalling that the company also finds its roots in Giannoni's training in psychology and in his experience as an art therapist using street performance to work with the homeless.[20] Before being a poet who tried to heal through both the printed and embodied word, the founder of maelstrÖm had trained in the tradition of Milton H. Erickson (1901–80) and family systems therapy,[21] which might in part explain Giannoni's emphasis on embeddedness in the community as well as his faith in art both tapping into and working on the subconscious.[22] For him as a creator and performer, one of the direct consequences of his grounding in psychotherapy is his absolute differentiation between the 'ego' and 'self': contrary to many forms of art and performance that, Giannoni believes, only aim at consolidating the 'ego', what maelstrÖm seeks to individuate is this far more fluctuating entity called the 'self', in which the physical, social, psychological and spiritual all coalesce into one.[23]

In line with Blake's own spiritual conception of art as intended to transform a manifold 'personhood' that exceeds the 'ego', the notions of *transmutation* and *transition* are at the heart of the many performances in word, song and dance that each year inform maelstrÖm's fiEstival and its curious blend of a mood of (re-)enchantment with a sense of apocalypse, reminiscent of the Blakean interplay between 'Innocence' and 'Experience', on the one hand, and the uncanny sense of expectation that accompanies regeneration and perceptual expansion at the end of Blake's major Prophetic Books, on the other. Together with the various workshops and meetings with writers/artists organised around them, these performances are not a mere juxtaposition of separate events, but rather represent different stages in one and the same spiritual and mythopoetic journey over four days, as already revealed by the titles chosen for the festival each year. From the Buddhist 'Koan of Emptiness' (2010) and Kabbalah-based 'Tree of Life' (2016) to the Tarot-inspired 'Arcana of Strength' (2017) and alchemical 'Songs of Transition. Movement 1: The Athanor' (2021), the maelstrÖm fiEstival operates as a kind of pilgrimage-in-*poiesis*, an always evolving concept intended to establish a momentary but deeper sense of community, together with a destabilising of normal perception of the space–time continuum.[24]

Beyond an inventive re-appropriation of urban space, defamiliarisation through an intensifying of the moment – be it in painful or celebratory aspects – is one of the threads unifying many of maelstrÖm's apparently heterogeneous sets of performances and poetic actions, it being hoped that the resulting euphoria or dizziness will help 'to make the invisible visible' again.[25] One of the most spectacular instances of this defamiliarisation occurred during the thirteenth fiEstival (2019) and its 'Journey through the Night', during which, raga-style, poetry was read, chanted and improvised over twelve consecutive hours from midnight to noon the next day.[26] Whether as gentle medicine or a powerfully vatic tool, *poiesis* and its defamiliarising potential are, for maelstrÖm, a path of perceptual healing leading, in Bertoli's Blake-like and esoteric formulation, to the moment when 'the rose cultivated in the soil becomes the one cultivated in the heart, when the instrumental means and utilitarianism of rationality are defeated by the pulsation of life'.[27]

Different Avenues of Dialogue with Blake: The Beat Generation

When it comes to Blake's legacy within maelstrÖm's search for this 'pulsation', the Beat Generation has played a major role in allowing Giannoni and other poets around him to access the work of the English visionary. Indeed, not only are Beat-affiliated authors well represented in maelstrÖm's catalogue of poetry in translation, but in certain cases, this translation enterprise has also gone hand in hand with sustained personal contact and actual participation in successive iterations of the fiEstival. In the formative years of the company, maelstrÖm also benefited from Bertoli's launch of an Italian version of City Lights in Florence in 1996. In its wake, Bertoli encouraged conversations between Giannoni and various Beat figures, including Tuli Kupferberg (1923–2010), whose band, The Fugs, had set Blake to music.[28] These exchanges with Beat-affiliated voices proved vital in opening even more widely the routes leading to Blake that members of maelstrÖm had begun to travel in their own private reading.

To understand the role played for maelstrÖm by the Beat Generation, one needs to distinguish four different strands in the complex web of interaction linking Blake and American counterculture after the Second World War: a) poetry as a tool of vision and consciousness expansion; b) poetry as the vehicle for ecstatic trance, often performed live; c) poetry as subversion of normative values through irreverence and the paradoxical interplay of opposites; and d) poetry as rebellion against any form of oppression and imperialism.

For Giannoni personally, it was The Doors (1965–73) and frontman Jim Morrison (1943–71) who led to the Beat Generation, not the reverse.[29] Most especially, it was through the band's name that the founder of maelstrÖm discovered its connection to Aldous Huxley's *The Doors of Perception* (1954) and its title alluding to *The Marriage of Heaven and Hell* (composed 1790).[30] In turn, this Morrison–Huxley–Blake chain made Giannoni aware of Beat subculture and its early interest in psychedelic exploration. In particular, it is through The Doors that Giannoni and others around him became familiar with the Blake-inspired poetry of Allen Ginsberg (1926–97), most especially 'Sunflower Sutra' (1956), and with Ginsberg's lifelong neo-shamanic calling, a vocation catalysed by the multiple moments of ecstasy triggered in 1948 by his reading of 'Ah! Sunflower', 'The Sick Rose', 'The Little Girl Lost/Found' diptych, and 'The Human Abstract'.[31] So in symbiosis with mentoring voices outside American counterculture, the creative ferment of The Doors leading to Blake and then to Ginsberg strengthened the early intuition of Giannoni and his acolytes: poets in contemporary society should make the mission of expansion of consciousness their own.

Within the Beat Generation, it was thus Ginsberg's link to Blake that confirmed the neo-shamanic potential of written *poiesis* as a tool for altering perception by loosening the shackles of materialism – understood both in the philosophical and consumerist sense. Yet, when it came to the power of the word in performance – be it with or without musical accompaniment – it is second-generation Beat poet Anne Waldman (b. 1945) who has, for maelstrÖm, most embodied the poet as neo-shamanic singer able to induce a trance-like state for performer and audience alike. Besides singing Blake on stage,[32] Waldman also makes no mystery of the importance she attributes to him as a spiritual teacher for the contemporary individual.[33] In repeated live collaborations with maelstrÖm,[34] Waldman can be seen to give tangible shape to the poet of double-edged Blakean madness, the one who frenetically plunges into evil to squarely contemplate 'Error', whilst simultaneously opening a breach in the mass of perceptual delusion to substitute liberatory ecstasy for painful insanity.[35] Significantly, Giannoni repeatedly refers in conversation to Waldman as a 'living shaman'.[36] Neither is it coincidental that two of the central items in maelstrÖm's catalogue are the French translations of *Fast Speaking Woman* (1975; trans. 2008) and *Jaguar Harmonics* (2014; trans. 2019): as two works exploring the neo-shamanic voice both thematically and aesthetically, they abound in litany-like repetitions and a frenzied accumulation of 'dissipative structures',[37] whereby Waldman transforms space–time on stage into what Blakean critics would deem an equivalent of Los's furnace of the mind, her percussive wielding of the spoken word reminiscent of his archetypal hammering subduing 'spectres'.[38]

If, for Giannoni and others, Waldman has embodied Blake's archetypal 'therapoet' in performance, it is Ferlinghetti who, at the political level, has particularly galvanised the collective, with works like *Blind Poet* (pub. and trans. 2004), *A Coney Island of the Mind* (1958; trans. 2008) and *Poetry as Insurgent Art* (2007; trans. 2012), all published in French translation by maelstrÖm. As a political testament akin to a contemporary 'Bible of Hell', *Poetry as Insurgent Art* and its Blakean spirit continue to legitimise the group's sense of poetic mission. Ferlinghetti's legendary talent for self-derision may have little in common with Blake's legacy, but the dialectic and provocative form of his aphorisms definitely does, as foreshadowed by the opening of his manifesto:

> I am signaling you through the flames.
> The North Pole is not where it used to be.
> Manifest Destiny is no longer manifest.
> ...
> What are poets for, in such an age?
> What is the use of poetry?
> The state of the world calls out for poetry to save it.[39]

Ferlinghetti's challenging credos, in which political radicalism and a deconditioning of the senses are co-dependent, well exceed the subversive energies of Surrealism alone. As in the last three lines quoted above, some aphorisms in *Poetry as an Insurgent Art* reflect upon the function and status of art in a manner possibly – if distantly – analogous to Blake's sustained probing into such questions for his own age in the *Laocoön* (composed *c*.1815, *c*.1826–27).[40] However, with much greater directness and certainty, they bring to mind the rebellious inversion of values of the *Marriage* as well as its irreverent dialectic play on contraries as the necessary source of progression. Moreover, *Poetry as Insurgent Art* reflects another Blakean hallmark of Ferlinghetti's output as a whole: a political radicalism whose corrosiveness does not undermine the wonder generated by ordinary particulars, but which paradoxically draws added strength from the ability to see the miraculous in them, since 'A sunflower maddened with light sheds the seeds of the poem. Some sprout.'[41]

For maelstrÖm, the punch of Ferlinghetti's political rebellion is complemented by the even more radical dissent of Jack Hirschman (1933–2021). Hirschman not only published a long poem about Blake in 1967,[42] but as one of the most emblematic figures of countercultural protest on the West Coast since the 1950s, perhaps best embodies the version of the neo-shamanic poet as 'prophet against empire', to borrow David Erdman's well-known phrase.[43] Indeed, after being fired from UCLA in 1965 for helping students to avoid the draft during the Vietnam War, Hirschman turned his back upon what he calls the 'corporation' of conventional academia to lead a nomadic life as a politically committed poet, artist and translator.[44] It is as iconic incarnations of what might, by analogy, be referred to as the poet of 'Spiritual Strife' opposing literal warmongering that both Hirschman and his French translator, poet Gilles B. Vachon (b. 1932), were the guests of honour celebrated at the 2016 maelstrÖm fiEstival.[45]

This 'Tree of Life' festival in fact coincided with the inclusion of Hirschman's *The Viet Arcane* (2014; trans. 2016) in maelstrÖm's catalogue, a neo-shamanic work in more respects than one: as a polyphonic esoteric work inspired by the Kabbalah and by the Vietnamese shamanic ritual of Len Dong, *The Viet Arcane* functions like a poetic Tarot pack of thirty-six symbolic characters whose successive incantations plunge the reader into the chaos of war in order to better exorcise it.[46] In its distortion of normal space–time, *The Viet Arcane* not only doubles as a poem and actual performance script, but also pushes to new extremes the Blakean notion of double-edged madness. Indeed, the chaos that kills is also the disorder that in the end heals, as revealed by concluding lines whose prosody nevertheless still bears the instability and scars of battle:

> This very clear day
> when we breathe in
> the glory of being
> united North & South
> and as a People
> …
> my wings glide
> …
> and descend into
> the body of the song
> sounding out of the mouth
> of the future[47]

It is thus as the creator of a contemporary equivalent to Blake's mythopoetic transmutation of destructive political conflict into a war of reintegration of the spirit that, as a major figure of the post-1945 American counterculture, Hirschman inspires maelstrÖm and the way it has been tapping into Blake's legacy.

Different Avenues of Dialogue with Blake: Influences and Confluences outside the Beat Generation

If the Beat Generation's productions have enabled Giannoni to deepen his appreciation of Blake, Beat voices did not so much bring about a first-time revelation as a *rediscovery* of Blake as archetype of the neo-shamanic poet. As explained to me in a personal interview, Giannoni's more thorough re-reading of Blake via the Beats in adulthood was preceded by a number of more minor encounters.[48] Giannoni readily admits that he was a relative latecomer to 'serious' literature, preferring science fiction instead as an adolescent. However, biblical narratives as told by the local priest had already fascinated him in childhood, giving him an important point of entry into Blake's Prophetic Books, which he would come across as an adult.

Though Giannoni did not directly read Blake in school, Edgar Allan Poe (1809–49), Jorge Luis Borges (1899–1986), Dante Alighieri (1265–1321) and Samuel Taylor Coleridge (1772–1834) were the electrifying literary encounters that helped to put Blake on his poetic radar. Whether Poe was directly influenced by Blake remains a matter open to debate.[49] By contrast, on top of lecturing and writing on the English visionary, Borges directly alluded in his own highly intertextual and labyrinth-like poetry to Blake's presence and influence.[50] One of these allusions is the reference to 'Blake's tiger of fire' found in the poem 'The Gold of Tigers', a 1972 piece included in Borges's poetry collection by the same name.[51] It was via 'The Gold of Tigers' that the teenage Giannoni first became aware of Blake's *Songs*.

The reading of Dante in upper-secondary school further prepared Giannoni for his receptivity to Blake's illustrations to *The Divine Comedy* (composed 1824–27), reproductions of which he chanced upon before his arrival in Belgium in 1987, though he cannot remember the exact date and context of this first, fortuitous encounter with Blake's visual work. Nevertheless, it is his illustrations to Dante that Giannoni unhesitatingly cites as his main connection to Blake's visual production. Beyond Dante, Giannoni considers that it was actually Coleridge in his sublimity 'who most conditioned [his] access to Blake' later on at university,[52] where he also discovered Milton's *Paradise Lost* (1667) and became aware of the fact that Blake had illustrated the poem.[53]

Giannoni's Italian contemporary and mentor, Bertoli, played an important role in introducing the founder of maelstrÖm to Romanticism at large and to Blake in particular. As Giannoni recalls, Bertoli often mentioned Blake, whose work he knew quite well since, besides popularising and publishing the Beat Generation in Italy, Bertoli had also lectured on avant-garde literatures at the University of Bologna.[54] In other words, Bertoli had taught classes on groups of radical innovators who, both inside and outside Italy, were deeply marked by Blake and sought to reappropriate him as the archetype of the visionary in touch with the forces of the unconscious leading to surreal perception.[55] Bertoli thus did more than act as an intermediary between Giannoni and the Beats: he guided him in his readings of the *Songs of Innocence and of Experience* and the *Marriage*, the two collections that Giannoni admits having studied most in depth, feeling a particular 'human closeness' to the latter.[56]

Unsurprisingly in view of the intellectually nomadic turn of mind characterising maelstrÖm, Giannoni does not see Blake as an exclusive source of psycho-spiritual teaching and inspiration, but as a major presence in a kind of 'esoteric family' whose members all approach life as a journey of initiation and re-attuning of energies in order to bring the fragments of being back into its original unity. In this nexus of cross-fertilisations and converging paths, Blake actually complements for Giannoni the all-important legacies of the French Surrealist poet René Daumal (1908–44), the Russian philosopher and mystic George Ivanovich Gurdjieff (1866/72/77–1949), and the Chilean film director and Tarot specialist Jodorowsky, already mentioned as one of the seminal influences on the creation of maelstrÖm.[57]

Daumal explicitly mentions Blake only once in his correspondence,[58] but as a member of the dissident Surrealist group *Le Grand Jeu* (1927–32), he had undoubtedly heard of him through other Surrealists like poet and painter Philippe Soupault (1897–1990)[59] or poet Roger Gilbert-Lecomte (1907–43).[60] Far more importantly, though, Daumal pursued a quest for mental deconditioning rooted in Blake-like axioms such as 'To perceive is not a fact: it is an investigation. There is no investigation for imaginary things', 'The virtuous man rejoices at being one-eyed', or 'Nature's law does not tire at bowing before its dead aunt.'[61] In his visionary questioning of narrow empiricism, Daumal, moreover, cultivated a Surrealist style whose irreverent incongruities nevertheless share an important commonality with the paradoxical dynamics of the *Marriage*: the subversion of accepted values through the provocative play on contraries. With evocative titles like *Se dégager du scorpion imposé* ('To Free Oneself from the Imposed Scorpion') or *Poème à Dieu et à l'Homme* ('Poem to God and Man'), Daumal's own 'Bibles of Hell' come complete with percussive aphorisms and sterile angels rebuked for their alleged purity, all this in an effort to reveal 'that All deities reside in the human breast'.[62]

Daumal became a disciple of Gurdjieff,[63] whose developmental philosophy meant to unify body, mind and emotions outside institutionally established religions. Gurdjieff's so-called 'Fourth Way'[64] has greatly nourished Giannoni and complemented his psychotherapeutic training in the Ericksonian school, as well as his initiation via Jodorowsky into the self-empowering symbolism of the Tarot.[65] Though the convergences between Gurdjieff and Blake should be discussed more in terms of *confluence* than influence, confluences probably facilitated by the theosophical context in which Gurdjieff matured, both mystics meet in considering that the human being needs to be awakened out of perceptual slumber in order to attain a higher form of awareness.[66] In turn, similar Blakean echoes pervade Jodorowsky's exploration of the Tarot as a symbolic, mandala-like tool of contemplation whereby blocked energies can be diagnosed and allowed to flow again.[67] Indeed, in line with Blakean mottoes like 'Energy is Eternal Delight'[68] and 'Expect poison from the standing water',[69] Jodorowsky sees all forms of illness as the result of physical, sexual, emotional or intellectual stagnation.[70]

maelstrÖm and Blake's Art of Totality and Spiritual War

Other prolific voices within the arts collective, such as the Luxembourg-born poet Tom Nisse (b. 1973) and the French poet Tom Buron (b. 1992), also openly admit to being influenced by Blake, again as a figure amidst a larger family of personal mentors. Within maelstrÖm, their respective Blakean trajectory is precious not only because of the extent to which it confirms Giannoni's own, but also due to how it differs from it.

Nisse's self-made pantheon is extremely varied, his influences ranging from Friedrich Hölderlin (1770–1843), Arthur Rimbaud (1854–91) and Georg Trakl (1887–1914) to bebop, The Doors and Bob Dylan (b. 1941).[71] Besides, as a multilingual poet, scholar and translator of German authors, Nisse has also undertaken in-depth research into most of the historical avant-gardes.[72] If the reading of 'The Tyger' and 'Ah! Sunflower' in secondary school paralleled his discovery of Ginsberg's poetry, Nisse's early interest in Blake was also reinforced by his listening to The Fugs and their setting of Blake to music. Another pivotal moment for Nisse was his viewing of *Dead Man* (1995),[73] the film directed by Jim Jarmusch

(b. 1953), which features a central hero named Blake to signal the work's indebtedness to the English visionary's ideals and poetics. Jarmusch's film represents such an iconic masterpiece for Nisse that it even inspired one of his poems, 'Le Film canoë' (2016).[74]

Generally, though, apart from the musicality and freedom of tone of the *Songs*, Nisse does not consider that Blake so much shaped his style as opened his mind to a philosophical world-view in which the poet must approach reality as a *totality* in which all dimensions are *interdependent*, from the spiritual to the social or from the sensory to the political.[75] It is because of Blake's plunging into the totality of being and its fundamentally interrelated nature that his ideals of freedom-within-solidarity crucially complement the historical avant-gardes and their influence on Nisse. Indeed, for him, libertarian ideals running counter to the mind's 'imprisonment via screens and clocks' go hand in hand with a search for social justice in an ecologically sustainable community, one including all forms of life.[76] Precisely with regard to his environmental awareness, Nisse remains as fascinated today as in youth by the sublimity of 'The Tyger' and the mysterious beauty of the non-human 'Other' it evokes.[77]

Next to the poet of *totality in interrelation*, it is also Blake the poet of *intensity* who impresses Nisse: when preparing a speech on the historical avant-gardes in 2016, Nisse turned to the Romantics as precursors and discovered the Englishman's visual work.[78] In it, Blake's '(mastered) rage of expression',[79] leading the viewer to a kind of vertigo in its transformation of ordinary time and space, came as a stunning revelation for Nisse: 'As a performer, it is perhaps the attempt to provoke a physical, sensory and emotional dizziness, one shared by artist … and audience, that brings me close to Blake's approach and undertaking.'[80]

Recognising Blake's notion of 'Spiritual Strife' in his own summons to self-directed internal warfare ('fais-toi la guerre'),[81] Buron too sheds interesting light on the poet of totality, intensity and mastered rage that Blake embodies for him.[82] Just like Giannoni and Nisse, his discovery of Blake started in adolescence, more specifically with his reading of the 1922 translation of the *Marriage* by André Gide (1869–1951), followed by a discovery of the Englishman's visual work thanks to the huge retrospective exhibition held in 2009 at the Grand Palais in Paris. For Buron too, the impact of these first encounters with Blake was greatly amplified via The Doors leading to the Beat Generation. Like Giannoni and Nisse, Buron has never considered Blake as a formative influence in isolation, but sees him as part of a set of complementary tutelary figures.

In this personal pantheon, Buron associates Blake first and foremost with Rimbaud and Friedrich Nietzsche (1844–1900) in a kind of 'infernal trio' embodying the refusal of established morality and truth, on the one hand, and the salvatory plunge into madness on the other.[83] For the young French poet as well, the latter constitutes a necessary step in the 'spiritual war' that individuals must wage internally with themselves in order to integrate, Buron particularly valuing Blake's idea of the fourfold human being.[84] It is precisely because of his 'mysticism of insanity' that Blake exerts so strong a fascination upon the author of *Nadirs* (2019):[85] in his eyes, like Rimbaud and Nietzsche, Blake embodies the ideal of the imaginative mind which 'accepts duelling and struggling with the demons',[86] and which subverts received morality by exploring 'Hell as a territory of the Dionysiac and not of punishment'.[87] This explains why, next to the *Songs*, the *Marriage* has remained to this day a constant reference for Buron. This also sheds light on why the young Frenchman has explored more deeply certain other sections of the Prophetic Books, in particular 'Night the Ninth' of *Vala* – Blakean texts in which the verse fluctuates between visionary dream and nightmare, with no reassuring boundaries between the two.[88]

Psychomachy, 'Bibles of Hell', and 'Perennial Wisdom'

Buron's full embrace of Blake's call to 'spiritual war' against the conventional ego offers important keys to his recently completed poetic triptych, *Nadirs* (2019), a psychomachy in which the acute psycho-spiritual struggle of the self translates as repeated plunges into the maelstrom of insanity.[89] The influence of Blake may be difficult to disentangle from that of Nietzsche, Rimbaud, or even Kerouac and Ginsberg. Indeed, the first two parts of *Nadirs*, 'Timbales téléphoniques' ('Telephone Timpani') and 'Nostaljukebox', show more than one parallel with Kerouac's *Mexico City Blues* (1959) and its processual spiritual labyrinth. In turn, part three, 'Le Blues du 21ème siècle' ('Twenty-first Century Blues') recalls the long-line catalogue of double-edged Blakean madness found in 'Howl', particularly in the latter's first and second sections of descent into a hellish reality. Beyond the occasional direct allusion to Blake, this neo-shamanic take on double-edged madness is precisely what makes Buron's triptych a fundamentally Blake-inflected whole.[90] In *Nadirs*, the poetic voice engages in a war against itself by trying to transform the alienation of the soul into healing ecstasy. It does so particularly by subverting the neat conventional boundaries between good and evil, the pure and the impure, and the holy and the profane, in a manner reminiscent of Blake's *Marriage* and its 'Proverbs of Hell'. In fact, the nadirs evoked in Buron's title are similarly twofold: if they correspond to the most abject levels of madness to which the soul wilfully accepts to sink, they also match the lowest degree to which ordinary perception needs to be brought in order for the self to resurface out of disintegration.

Buron's mythopoetic journey of self-initiation is not an isolated example in maelstrÖm's publishing catalogue. *Ghost Words* (2011) by Olivier Dombret (b. 1980), *Ouroboros* (2008) by Damien Spleeters (b. 1986), or *Derrière les paupières … l'immensité* ('Behind the Eyelids … Immensity', 2019) by CeeJay (1946–2020) are examples of other psychomachies that rely on a neo-shamanic voice straddling the poetic and the philosophical in its inner pilgrimage and spiritual warfare. In a different register altogether, there is also the Tarot-inspired *La Face cachée de la ville* ('The Hidden Face of the City', 2010–12), Giannoni's collaboration with graphic artist Daniele Bacci (b. 1962) that resulted in a neo-shamanic cartoon thriller. Its hero, Inspector Colon,[91] is made to journey between dimensions with the aid of Juan-Maria, a shaman disguised as a tramp, who bequeaths to him a totem spirit in the form of a tapir named Chris.[92] Not only do the overlapping universes of the spiritually named city in its real, utopian and dystopian forms – present Bramacity, past Bramapan, and future Bramaryan respectively – offer fortuitous parallels with Blake's own psychogeography, but in addition, both hero and reader are also repeatedly reminded that the multiple outward journeys are but an inner one: 'wherever you will go, Colon, whatever you will search for, it is only yourself that you will find'.[93]

Like *Nadirs*, all these works function in print as an arena of mental deconditioning through the unsettling of the normal perception of space–time akin to the one that maelstrÖm repeatedly tries to offer in actual performance. Like *Nadirs* too, these journeys of initiation in print may contain occasional intertextual allusions to Blake, but it is not this feature which fundamentally makes them partake of Blake's spirit: rather, as suggested by the title of one of Giannoni's mythopoetic labyrinths, *Oeil Ouvert, Oeil Fermé* ('Open Eye, Closed Eye', 2007), such works encourage the 'unlearning' of habitual perception through the 'physical eye' only, or what Blake calls 'the Vegetated Mortal Eye's perverted and single vision'.[94]

In their intention to open the reader's 'third' or 'imaginative' eye, some of the neo-shamanic texts produced by maelstrÖm are far more openly didactic in their straddling of poetry and philosophy. As such, they fall into a category labelled '*Poésophie*' in the publishing catalogue of the arts collective, the portmanteau neologism limpidly conveying the idea that, in keeping with the ancient roots of poetry as a vehicle of the sacred, contemporary verse is still a gateway to 'perennial wisdom'. Often as explicitly didactic as they are implicitly Gnostic, these texts, like Blake's *Marriage*, revel in the power of awakening and instruction of the aphoristic paradox and subversive play on contraries. Next to Giannoni's own *La Foi et la connaissance* ('Faith and Knowledge', 2016), there are, for instance, also his translations into French of Jodorowsky's *De aquello que no se puede hablar* ('Of That Which Remains Unsayable', 2002) and Bertoli's *Astri e disastri: Canti dalla transizione* ('Stars and Disasters: Songs of Transition', 2016). In general, like the *Songs* and the *Marriage*, these works seek to reveal through an oxymoronic logic and provocative inversion of accepted values, but sometimes Blake's presence is felt more directly in these manuals of 'spiritual warfare':

> La formidable importance que l'on attribue à être un tigre
> ne revient pas à posséder la clé maîtresse mais
> un vulgaire crochet
> or, en assumant le rôle d'un agneau tondu et innocent
> nous obtiendrons un miroir qui nous permette d'accepter
> que cette triste image que nous sommes en train
> de contempler
> n'est ni plus ni moins que celle d'une divinité solitaire.
>
> [The formidable importance given to being a tiger
> does not boil down to possessing the main key but
> only a vulgar lock pick

yet, by taking on the part of a shorn and innocent lamb,
we will obtain a mirror that allows us to accept
that this sad image we are
contemplating
is neither more nor less than that of a solitary divinity.][95]

Recycling Blake's tiger of Experience and lamb of Innocence, Jodorowsky produces an updated version of 'All deities reside in the human breast',[96] bringing the proverb's meaning closer to what Jean Claude Bologne (b. 1956) calls a 'mysticism without God'.[97]

Conclusion

Though the name 'maelstrÖm reEvolution' actually derives from Poe, the churning forces it evokes nevertheless resonate with Blake's notion of the 'vortex', as well as with his neo-shamanic conception of healing that involves journeying between an alternatively alienating and ecstatic version of madness.[98] Furthermore, the name of the Brussels-based arts collective ties in with the processual turbulence inherent in Blake's 'spiritual war' within a fourfold 'self' always seeking to hold in balance the Imagination, intellect, emotions and the body, as well as striving to bridge personal and social transformation.[99]

Blake's mythopoetic plunge into double-edged madness and its analogies to traditional shamanic healing have continued to speak across cultures to writers and artists refusing to bury the spiritual nature of the creative process as well as the ensuing social relevance of the artist for their community. Giannoni and his acolytes within maelstrÖm clearly situate themselves in this lineage: be it in print or performance, their 'therapoetry' both reflects and is driven by Blake's iconic embodiment of the poet as shaman, on the one hand, and the interpenetration of the artistic, therapeutic and spiritual processes in his work on the other. This is why Blake belongs to the larger 'esoteric family' of figures who have inspired maelstrÖm as heirs to the counterculture of the Long Sixties, with its paradoxical blend of rupture with the past and renewed anchorage in various, cross-fertilising forms of 'perennial wisdom'. Be it through the Beat Generation or through other sources, for maelstrÖm reEvolution, the limited territory defined by the physical boundaries of its bookstore and its fiEstival supports a far wider one defying all borders and languages: the territory of *poiesis* as a healing, trance-inducing tool that not only leads to spiritual transformation, but also, indeed, to a 'mysticism without God'.

Notes

1 I wish to extend my warmest thanks to David Giannoni, Tom Buron and Tom Nisse, who so generously gave of their time to help me in my reflection on the Blake–maelstrÖm dialogue. Without the inspiring exchanges with them, this article would simply not have matured as it did. Their kindness and generosity are all the more remarkable as they agreed to share their insights in a very troubled period for the arts in Belgium,

COVID-19 having deprived many poets of the opportunity to perform live, if not of their livelihood. I also owe special thanks to poet and René Daumal specialist Zéno Bianu, who took time out from his own writing projects to answer my queries regarding the possible links between Blake and Daumal. Finally, I would also like to thank the anonymous peer reviewer for some very helpful insights and suggestions.

2 The term is here understood in the sense of 'displacement, mental distraction, astonishment, trance', based on its ancient Greek etymology 'to cause to stand out of'. It should be kept in mind that as 'a state of being beyond reason and self-control', ecstasy can be equally close to pain and violent transport as to rapture and delight. See www.merriam-webster.com/dictionary/ecstasy (accessed 2 March 2021).

3 M. Harner, 'What is a Shaman?', in G. Doore (ed.), *Shaman's Path: Healing, Personal Growth, & Empowerment* (Boston and London: Shambala, 1988), pp. 7–8, 11.

4 J. Achterberg, 'The Wounded Healer', in Doore (ed.), *Shaman's Path*, pp. 119–21.

5 M. Wilson, *The Life of William Blake* (1927; London: Granada Publishing, 1978), pp. 73–80.

6 W. Blake, *The Marriage of Heaven and Hell* (plate 14), in D. Erdman (ed.), *The Complete Poetry and Verse of William Blake* (New York: Doubleday, 1988), p. 39. Following the conventions of Blake scholarship, passages from Erdman's edition of Blake's verse subsequently referenced as E followed by page number.

7 A. Ostriker, 'Blake, Ginsberg, Madness, and the Prophet as Shaman', in R. J. Bertholf and A. S. Levitt (eds), *William Blake and the Moderns* (Albany: State University of New York Press, 1982), pp. 114, 117–18, 128.

8 W. Blake, *Jerusalem* (plate 12), E155.

9 Ostriker, 'Blake, Ginsberg, Madness', pp. 117–18, 128.

10 *Ibid.*, pp. 114–18.

11 W. Blake, 'Annotations to Spurzheim's *Observations on Insanity*', *The Marginalia*, E663.

12 R. Pattee, 'Ecstasy and Sacrifice', in Doore (ed.), *Shaman's Path*, p. 24.

13 L. E. Mehl, 'Modern Shamanism: Integration of Biomedicine with Traditional World Views', in Doore (ed.), *Shaman's Path*, pp. 129–30.

14 *Ibid.*

15 Pattee, 'Ecstasy and Sacrifice', p. 24.

16 In conversation, Giannoni often refers to himself not merely as a poet but as a '*thérapoète*' ('therapoet'). As rarely used in French as in English, '*thérapoésie*' and 'therapoetry' are nevertheless very meaningful recent neologisms: as suggested by the portmanteau coinage and its fusion of the concepts of 'therapy' and 'poetry', 'therapoetry' powerfully expresses the healing function of art and its fundamental importance in helping individuals and communities to overcome mental illness and psychological fracture. Thus, the term 'therapoetic' not only invites further research into the still poorly understood curative functions of the poetic, but it also reminds us of ancient notions such as catharsis and its purifying of the emotions in the theatre of Ancient Greece.

17 A. Bertoli, 'Terapia di Analfabetizzazione/Thérapie d'Analphabétisation', in A. Bertoli, *Thérapie d'analphabétisation/Terapia di analfabetizzazione*, trans. D. Giannoni (Brussels: maelstrÖm reEvolution, 2010), pp. 18–19.

18 For full details of the company's birth and development, see F. Bellarsi, 'Transmuting Energies in the Belgian Francophone Matrix: MaelstrÖm ReEvolution or the Brussels Reincarnation of the Beat Spirit', in A. R. Lee (ed.), *The Routledge Handbook of International Beat Literature* (New York and London: Routledge, 2018), pp. 129–43.

19 *Ibid.*, pp. 131–3.

20 Immediately after his arrival in Belgium in 1987, Giannoni embarked upon a degree in psychology at the francophone university of Louvain.

21 F. Bellarsi, interview with D. Giannoni (Brussels, 25 January 2021).

22 The Ericksonian approach heavily relies on (auto-)hypnosis for healing, that is, on states partly akin to trance and ecstasy. In addition, Ericksonians also conceive of therapeutic action in terms of dramaturgical set-up and artistic strategies. See, for instance, Jeffrey K. Zeig, 'The (Dramatic) Process of Psychotherapy', *The American Journal of Clinical Hypnosis*, 51 (2008), 41–55. In particular, Zeig, one of Erickson's direct heirs, explains that, like dramatists, 'Practitioners of hypnosis learn to use many unusual microdynamic methods to alter experience and modify the level of perceived tension. ... Hypnosis is a technology of impact, not of understanding. The essential purpose of hypnosis is to evoke experiential change; ... Dramaturgy has influenced human behavior more than psychotherapy. Psychotherapists would do well to study methods that dramatists use. The art of drama is the art of having impact' (pp. 43, 54). Such statements make it easier to understand why the boundaries between the therapist, artist and performer tend to thin for someone like Giannoni when it comes to working on the subconscious in an effort to solve the problem, as Zeig again puts it, 'that people *know*, but they do not *realize* what they know' (p. 54).

23 *Ibid.*

24 'Le Kōan du Vide' (fiEstival #4); 'L'Arbre de vie' (fiEstival #10); 'L'Arcane de la Force' (fiEstival #11); 'Chants de la transition. 1er mouvement: L'Athanor' (fiEstival #15). For full details, see www.fiestival.net/fiestival/fiestivals-precedents.html and www.fiestival.net/programme-du-fiestival/programme-complet-du-fiestival.html (accessed 10 May 2021).

25 My translation, 'faire paraître l'invisible'. Epigraph to CeeJay, *Derrière les paupières ... l'immensité* (Amay: l'Arbre à paroles, 2019).

26 'La Traversée de la Nuit'. See 'reEvolution' (fiEstival #13), www.fiestival.net/fiestival/fiestivals-precedents/17-articles-fiestival-en-cours/562-la-traversee-de-la-nuit.html (accessed 13 May 2021).

27 My translation, 'quand la rose que l'on cultive dans la terre devient celle que l'on cultive dans le cœur, quand l'instrumentalité et l'utilitarisme de la rationalité sont défaits par la pulsation de vie'. A. Bertoli, 'Que faire d'une rose', in A. Bertoli, *Thérapie d'analphabétisation/Terapia di analfabetizzazione*, p. 35.

28 Bellarsi, 'Transmuting Energies', p. 132. It is on their debut album, *The Fugs Sing Ballads of Contemporary Protest, Points of View, and General Dissatisfaction* (Broadside Records, 1965), that the band co-founded by Ed Sanders (b. 1939) and Tuli Kupferberg adapted Blake's 'Ah! Sunflower' and 'How Sweet I Roam'd'.

29 Bellarsi, interview with D. Giannoni (2021).

30 Subsequently abbreviated as *Marriage* throughout the article.

31 Bellarsi, interview with D. Giannoni (2021); T. Clarke, 'Allen Ginsberg: The Paris Review Interview [1966]', in George Plimpton (ed.), *Beat Writers at Work. The Paris Review Interviews* (London: The Harvill Press, 1999), pp. 55–65. Though Ginsberg's accounts of his 1948 Blake-inspired visions vary in some details, the Clarke interview remains the best starting point to try and understand their complex significance.

32 See 'Anne Waldman Singing William Blake's "The Garden of Love" to Allen Ginsberg's Tune' (Washington Square Park, 2016), www.youtube.com/watch?v=lZwI5whrnBw (accessed 18 May 2021).

33 See V. Parakala, 'William Blake Is Important for Our Pedagogy, Says Poet Anne Waldman' (Jaipur Literary Festival: 2017), www.livemint.com/Leisure/ljtAjfFvBJbzpXW-xgRXsTL/William-Blake-is-important-for-our-Pedagogy-says-poet-Ann.html (accessed 10 April 2021).

34 See fiEstival #2 (2008), #4 (2010), #5 (2011), #8 (2014), #11 (2017) and #13 (2019). Waldman and Giannoni also performed together in Brussels on 29 October 2015 during the fourth annual meeting of the European Beat Studies Network held at the Université libre de Bruxelles.

35 W. Blake, *The Book of Los* (plate 4), E92; *The Four Zoas* (page 120), E390; *Jerusalem* (plates 41–2), E188–9.

36 F. Bellarsi, interview with D. Giannoni (Brussels, 27 May 2017).

37 A. Waldman, 'I Is Another: Dissipative Structures', in A. Waldman, *Fast Speaking Woman* (San Francisco: City Lights, 1996), pp. 127–8. Waldman borrows from the theories of physicist Ilya Prigogine (1917–2003) and sees verse as behaving by analogy to the instability and unpredictable order of the open systems of nature. It is this intersection between *poiesis* and certain aspects of chaos theory which in part accounts for the potential of poetry and performance to generate ecstatic states.

38 W. Blake, *Jerusalem* (plate 58; 91), E207–8; E251–2.

39 L. Ferlinghetti, *Poetry as Insurgent Art* (New York: New Directions, 2007), p. 3. Ferlinghetti was celebrated in maelstrÖm's fiEstival #2 (2008).

40 I wish to thank the peer reviewer for making me aware of this possibility. Whether we are dealing here with a case of mere confluence or straightforward influence remains open to debate and can only be explored elsewhere. However, as both a poet and visual artist, it is hard to imagine that Ferlinghetti was not aware of at least some of the aesthetic debates surrounding the Laocoön sculpture.

41 L. Ferlinghetti, *Americus: Book I* (New York: New Directions, 2004), p. 16.

42 J. Hirschman, *William Blake* (Topanga, CA: Love Press, 1967).

43 See D. Erdman, *Prophet against Empire: A Poet's Interpretation of the History of His Own Times* (Princeton, NJ: Princeton University Press, 1954).

44 J. Hirschman, 'A Miracle Book', in J. Hirschman, *L'Arcane du Viêt-Nam/The Viet Arcane*, trans. G. B. Vachon (Brussels: maelstrÖm reEvolution, 2016), p. 6.

45 W. Blake, *The Everlasting Gospel*, E520.

46 Hirschman, 'A Miracle Book', pp. 8–14. As he explains in these pages, Hirschman discovered Len Dong, a ritual linked to the 'Worship of the Great Mother' (p. 10), in the wake of his interest in Voodoo. In Len Dong too, song and dance are central methods to induce trances for a medium supposed to become possessed by the spirit of different

entities, including those of the forces of nature. See, for instance, '"Len Dong" rituals Shamans in Vietnam', www.youtube.com/watch?v=zJBeVUXwD4E (accessed 27 June 2021).

47 Hirschman, *L'Arcane du Viêt-Nam/The Viet Arcane*, pp. 258, 260.

48 Bellarsi, interview with D. Giannoni (2021).

49 See, for instance, K. J. Hayes, 'Poe's Knowledge of William Blake', *Notes and Queries*, 61 (2014), 83–4; J. B. Huma, 'Poe's "Ligea": Glanvill's Will or Blake's Will?', *Mississippi Quarterly: The Journal of Southern Cultures*, 26 (1973), 55–62.

50 See 'Borges sobre Blake', www.estacionlibro.com.ar/prologos/borges-sobre-blake/ (accessed 10 April 2021), and 'Borges profesor. Clase 15: William Blake. Blake y Swedenborg. Rupert Brooke. Poemas de Blake', https://borgestodoelanio.blogspot.com/2016/07/borges-profesor-clase-15-william-blake.html (accessed 10 April 2021).

51 J. L. Borges, 'L'Or des tigres', in J. L. Borges, *L'Or des tigres, L'Autre, le même II, Eloge de l'ombre, Ferveur de Buenos Aires*, trans. Ibarra (Paris: Gallimard, 2005), pp. 228–9.

52 My translation, 'qui a le plus conditionné mon accès à Blake', in Bellarsi, 'Interview Giannoni' (2021).

53 However, Giannoni did not have access to them and immersed himself instead in Gustave Doré's 1874 engravings of the same.

54 Bellarsi, interview with D. Giannoni (2021).

55 See the chapters on France, Belgium and Italy in S. Erle and M. D. Paley, *The Reception of William Blake in Europe* (London: Bloomsbury Academic, 2019).

56 My translation, 'une proximité humaine', in Bellarsi, interview with D. Giannoni (2021). Giannoni openly admits that the Prophetic Books continue to resist him – perhaps, paradoxically, because they might be too close to his own mythopoetic universe!

57 Due to varying autobiographical accounts, Gurdjieff's date of birth remains uncertain.

58 Z. Bianu, e-mail correspondence with F. Bellarsi (10 February 2021). In a letter dated 18 September 1928 and addressed to André Rolland de Renéville (1903–62), Daumal endorses the dissident Surrealist manifesto authored by his fellow poet. Daumal's letter includes *verbatim* de Renéville's document, which, in its defence of the spiritual side of Surrealism, lists Blake alongside Platonic doctrines, Poe's conception of the cosmos, the Kabbalah, and Rimbaud's works (p. 269). See René Daumal, *Correspondance I, 1915–1928*, ed. H. J. Maxwell (Paris: Gallimard, 1992), pp. 267–9.

59 Together with his wife, Marie-Louise, Soupault translated the *Songs* into French. See William Blake, *Chants d'innocence et d'expérience* (Paris: Editions des Cahiers libres, 1927). Within a series entitled 'Les Maîtres de l'art moderne' ('masters of modern art'), Soupault also authored an essay on Blake as a visual artist, soberly entitled *William Blake* (Paris: Les Editions Rieder, 1928).

60 In the inaugural issue of the dissident Surrealist journal *Le Grand Jeu*, to which Daumal himself contributed, his friend and acolyte, Gilbert-Lecomte, mentions Blake as having 'seen in the primordial night the last of the gods, the creative Madmen who were exhaling worlds' ('vu dans la nuit primordiale les derniers des dieux, les Fous créateurs, qui expiraient les mondes', pp. 13–14). See R. Gilbert-Lecomte, 'La Force des renoncements', *Le Grand Jeu*, 1 (1928), 12–18.

61 My translation, 'Percevoir n'est pas un fait: c'est une investigation. Il n'y a pas d'investigation pour les choses imaginaires'; 'L'homme vertueux se réjouit d'être borgne'; 'La loi de la nature ne se lasse pas de faire des courbettes devant sa tante la morte', in R. Daumal (*Se dégager du scorpion imposé*), *Poésies et notes inédites 1924–28*, ed. C. Rugafiori and A. Marangoni (Bastia: Eolienne, 2014), pp. 11, 68, 71.
62 Blake, *The Marriage of Heaven and Hell* (plate 11), E38.
63 Bellarsi, interview with D. Giannoni (2021).
64 See www.gurdjiefflegacy.org/70links/fourthway.htm (accessed 18 May 2021).
65 *Ibid.*
66 See J. Petsche, 'Gurdjieff and Blavatsky: Western Esoteric Teachers in Parallel', *Literature & Aesthetics*, 21 (2011), 98–115.
67 A. Jodorowsky, *La voie du tarot* (Paris: Albin Michel, 2004), p. 34.
68 Blake, *The Marriage of Heaven and Hell* (plate 4), E34.
69 *Ibid.* (plate 9), E37.
70 Jodorowsky, *La voie du tarot*, p. 34.
71 T. Nisse, Blake Questionnaire in email to F. Bellarsi (Brussels: 19 February 2021).
72 *Ibid.*
73 Nisse, Blake Questionnaire.
74 T. Nisse, *Extraire* (Amay: l'Arbre à paroles, 2016), pp. 27–30.
75 Nisse, Blake Questionnaire.
76 *Ibid.* My translation, 'l'incarcération par les écrans et les horloges'.
77 *Ibid.*
78 *Ibid.*
79 *Ibid.* My translation, 'rage (maîtrisée) d'expression'.
80 *Ibid.* My translation, 'En tant que performeur, c'est peut-être d'essayer de provoquer un vertige physique, sensoriel et émotionnel, partagé par l'artiste … et par le public, qui me rapproche de la démarche de Blake'.
81 Blake, *The Everlasting Gospel*, E520.
82 T. Buron, Blake Questionnaire in email to F. Bellarsi (Brussels: 3 February 2021).
83 *Ibid.*
84 *Ibid.*
85 *Ibid.* My translation, 'un mysticisme de la folie'.
86 *Ibid.* My translation, 'qui accepte le duel, le combat, avec les démons'.
87 *Ibid.* My translation, 'l'Enfer comme un territoire dionysiaque et non pas un territoire punitif'.
88 *Ibid.*
89 The expression 'fais-toi la guerre' or variants thereof punctuate Buron's text as, for instance, on pp. 137, 141, 153–4.
90 *Nadirs* includes an allusion to Blake's Jerusalem on p. 41: 'Je suis un locataire céleste, Sors-moi d'ici, / Montre-moi Jérusalem!' ('I am an occupant of heaven / Get me out of here / Show me Jerusalem'). Blake's 'Tyger' is also evoked on p. 43: 'ce félin qui donne la mesure de mes puretés évanouies / depuis un quart de siècle' ('this feline who has given full measure to my vanished purities / for the last quarter century'). Possibly, another

Blakean allusion occurs on p. 45 in the title of Section III, 'Sol Invictus', with its playful inversion of Los's name.

91 Interestingly, the inspector's surname, 'Colon', suggests travel and discovery at two levels, since in French, there is a homophonic ambiguity between the term for 'settler'/'colonist' and 'Colomb', the patronym of the explorer Colombus.

92 The names are again highly symbolic: the totem spirit suggests both Christ and Christopher, the patron saint of travellers, whereas the shaman's name is reminiscent of anthropologist Carlos Castaneda (1925–98) and his allegedly real Yaqui shaman Don Juan.

93 'Où que tu ailles, Colon, et quoi que tu cherches, c'est toi-même que tu trouves …', in D. Giannoni and D. Bacci, *La Face Cachée de la Ville: L'intégrale* (Brussels: maelstrÖm reEvolution, 2017), p. 76. Though the work presents interesting parallels with Blake's visual work and with Alan Moore's, both Giannoni and Bacci deny any direct influence and we must speak of confluence instead.

94 Blake, *Jerusalem* (plate 53), E202.

95 My translation of Giannoni's French version of the text, in A. Jodorowsky, *De ce dont on ne peut parler / De aquello que no se puede hablar* (Brussels: maelstrÖm reEvolution, 2002), p. 15.

96 Blake, *The Marriage of Heaven and Hell* (plate 11), E38.

97 See J. C. Bologne, *Une mystique sans Dieu* (Paris: Albin Michel, 2015). Interestingly, for his latest novel, *Le Nouvel An cannibale* ('The Cannibal New Year', 2021), Bologne chose as illustration for the cover Blake's *Nebuchadnezzar* (composed 1795, printed *c.*1805).

98 W. Blake, *Milton* (plate 15), E109.

99 'The Head Sublime, the Heart Pathos, the Genitals Beauty, the Hands & Feet Proportion', in Blake, *The Marriage of Heaven and Hell* (plate 10), E37.

EU authorised representative for GPSR:
Easy Access System Europe, Mustamäe tee 50,
10621 Tallinn, Estonia
gpsr.requests@easproject.com

www.ingramcontent.com/pod-product-compliance
Lightning Source LLC
LaVergne TN
LVHW061223100826
845148LV00004B/846

* 9 7 8 1 5 2 6 1 6 6 3 6 4 *